I Made a Booboo

A marketing professional with an MBA from Indian School of Business, Hyderabad, **Shivangi Sharma** has co-authored an anthology titled *Dutched Up* (rated among the top travel books of 2015 by *The Wall Street Journal*) and has written for *Mother's World*, a popular parenting magazine. She lives in Amsterdam with her husband, who plays way more sports than a normal wife can be okay with, and her son, who rarely listens to her. To maintain her sanity through it all, she performs as part of a professional Bollywood dance troupe in different European cities, and indulges in yoga, spirituality and music at home.

I Made a Booboo

A mom who had parenting all sorted...until she had a baby

SHIVANGI SHARMA

RUPA

Published by
Rupa Publications India Pvt. Ltd 2016
7/16, Ansari Road, Daryaganj
New Delhi 110002

Sales Centres:
Allahabad Bengaluru Chennai
Hyderabad Jaipur Kathmandu
Kolkata Mumbai

Copyright © Shivangi Sharma 2016

The views and opinions expressed in this book are the author's own and the facts are as reported by her which have been verified to the extent possible, and the publishers are not in any way liable for the same.

All rights reserved.
No part of this publication may be reproduced, transmitted, or stored in a retrieval system, in any form or by any means, electronic, mechanical, photocopying, recording or otherwise, without the prior permission of the publisher.

ISBN: 978-81-291-3880-4

First impression 2016

9 8 7 6 5 4 3 2 1

The moral right of the author has been asserted.

This book is sold subject to the condition that it shall not, by way of trade or otherwise, be lent, resold, hired out, or otherwise circulated, without the publisher's prior consent, in any form of binding or cover other than that in which it is published.

To my son, who proved every parenting book wrong and made me write one of my own.
If not for him, this book wouldn't have existed.
(Or perhaps it would have, but just like a Garfield comic strip without Garfield in it.)

Disclaimers

☆ This book won't teach you parenting—because no book can. It will tell you what it might look like.
☆ No babies were left unattended when this book was written. (They had iPads.*)
☆ Holy poop! I forgot what the third point was. Damn you, mommy-brain!

---

*Not really. Relax.

Contents

First Words   *xi*

The Beginning—the Best Place to Start	1
Stork Brings the Baby. Well, Not Exactly	17
So This Is What It Looks Like	28
Breakfast (and Lunch and Dinner) of Champions	42
Congratulations on Finishing Second in the Parenting Game. (So What If There Were Only Two Participants!)	52
Dearly Beloved Sleep, I Hope We Shall Meet Again Someday	66
The Day(s)care Saga or How Babies Trap You Out of Your Own Will	82
Guess Which Job Is Tougher? (Hint: It's the One Where You Don't Get Weekends Off)	98

Does It Get Easier? No, You Get Better at It	113
Meet the New Me, Who Is Nothing Short of Awesome (at Least While the Baby Sleeps)	127
His Majesty—the Invincible, the Unrestricted, the Toddler	145
It's Still Not the End. Neither Do I Want It to Be	169
An Apologia to My Son	187
Questions to Discuss with Other Parents	190
Appendix: The New Mommy Alphabet	191
Acknowledgements	195

First Words

Hi there, parents. How are you? Tired, but still going strong?

Remember when your weekends used to be full of three hour afternoon naps and sleeping in till late in the mornings?

Me neither.

But let me tell you, you are not alone. There is a virtual new parents' society that exists somewhere, and you were automatically affiliated to it when your little one was born. Today, I come before you as a representative of that society to remind you to sit back, brew yourself a cuppa and just tune out of everything. You deserve a break more than anyone else. I present to you my whirlwind journey as a first-time mom—one that is full of insane, unforgettable and goofed-up moments. You may find here: Things that you can relate to, things that will make you laugh and things that could possibly touch your hearts.

Hi there, parents-to-be. How are you? Excited, right?

First of all, congratulations on signing up for an experience that will shake you to the core—in a good way, of course. You might be bursting at your seams with advice from the whole world right now. But you really need to get into the water to learn how to swim and not just watch a YouTube video of swimming lessons. I will only say one thing—just take everything easy. As long as you don't serve them drugs, your children will turn out to be fine. And so will you. You only need a bit of freely available common sense and some love to get you through.

Hi there, whoever-does-not-fall-in-the-above-two-categories-of-people. How are you? Good, I hope?

If you want to know what you were as a small child, read this book. It might make you respect your parents a wee bit more. Or help you take a decision (either way) about your future procreating plans.*

---

*I can't be held responsible for anything, however. Just to give you an idea—this book has positive words like laugh, love and happy mentioned over 99 times, cry 74 times and poop about 20 times.

The Beginning—
the Best Place to Start

To reproduce is the most natural thing to do in this world for all species. But we are not birds or animals; we can easily crack the utterly distorted captcha codes in three attempts. And hence, we think. We think if we should have a baby, when we should have a baby, how many we should have, with whom we should have, where we should have, etc. Discounting for accidents, the common belief is that you should have one only if you really feel like it and can take the mountain of responsibility and hard work that comes along with it, head on. So before you go any further with this book, I would like you to take a quick test to see if you are the parenting type:

☆   Are you fine with counting out loud till three, with some extra excitement at three—more like '*thareeeeee*' at least 56 times a day? 'Let's sit in the car—one, two, *thareeeeeee.*' 'Let's stop sticking our heads out of the car window—one, two, *thareeeeee.*' It doesn't matter if the activity is not done after the counting; you start again, and with the same level of excitement as the first time.

☆ Are your feet strong enough to bear the excruciating pain of stepping on a Lego block while sleepwalking? Mind you, this is no mean feat. Only a parent knows where a toy pinches.

☆ Do you agree that wearing sparkling clean and ironed clothes to work is highly overrated? And that it is absolutely fine to clean your yogurt-stained black pants with a baby wipe when leaving for an important meeting? (After all, you *have* worn those pants twice before in the week, since everything else was dirty too, so it's not like you are not capable of sporting yogurt-free clothes.)

☆ Do you think it is morally right to insist on playing hide-and-seek with your kid, just so you can hide in the kitchen and gobble down some chips and/or chocolate? If not, then are you okay to permanently live with a little moocher who wants to eat whatever you are eating, whenever you are eating?

☆ Do you ever feel that you don't have anything to do on the weekends? That there is nothing on TV that you haven't watched before? That you are spending way too much time in the bathroom?

☆ Can you live with getting physically abused by a person a third your size every day and not being

able to do anything about it, not even yelling back?
- ☆ Are you a morning person? And a night person? And an afternoon and evening person? Basically, a person who is on call duty 24x7?
- ☆ (Philosophical question): Do you think that your life has no purpose?*
- ☆ (Practical question): Suspend a football from the roof with a string. Stick some faux hair on it. Now, give the ball a push so that it starts oscillating. Try giving that moving ball a haircut, without poking or harming it in any way. Were you successful? Of course, you can say you will have a hair dresser do that for your kid. Stop rolling your eyes now and roll that ball on the ground instead. And while the ball is still rolling, try to put pants on it. Were you successful this time?
- ☆ (Multiple choice question): What is your opinion of bodily fluids (not your own)?
  a) You don't mind dealing with them every day.
  b) You don't mind dealing with them every day.
  c) You don't mind dealing with them every day.
- ☆ Do you want to laugh your heart out; find happiness in the tiniest of things; release more endorphin than ever before; put yourself second, not because you have to but because you want to; love and be loved unconditionally and unfathomably; feel proud; cry

---

*About question 8: Having a baby will not give you a purpose in life, silly. It will just not give you enough time to ponder on such things anymore.

silly; spread your arms wide for a hug that can set everything right; feel like you have 'come home'; be elated; mean the world to someone and give a thousand kisses—all in the same day, every day?

That's it. End of quiz. If you answered yes to these questions (and attempted the multiple choice question), you have it in you to be a successful parent. So go ahead, there is a life waiting to be created by you—one that will teach you what life is actually about.

If you still have the book in your hands, you do seem serious about parenting. Good, so let's get on with the real stuff.

Typically, in about two to three years—and I say that based on my research of non-parent married couples around me—the novelty of marriage starts to diminish. You are still happily married, but now you are used to each other and their snoring like the family you grew up with. You no longer try to control your belches in front of each other and you may even discuss your gastrointestinal issues with your partner on a date night. The wedding DVD that you watched over and over again cosying up on the couch, catches dust in a corner and is only found when you move houses. Even then, the latest *Die Hard* is more fun to watch.

You don't necessarily have to do everything together now, so you stop faking your interest in husband's football match finals and wife's cruising through malls for aimless shopping. You are on an auto pilot—wake up, get ready, go to work, come home, eat, watch TV, sleep; with some socializing, grocery shopping, individual hobbies and spa visits on weekends. In your conscious attempt to give each other enough space, you have created a lot of room around you that can easily be utilized if tried.

Then you get invited to baby showers and first birthdays. The frosted cupcakes, the primary colours, the ridiculously tiny baby shoes and the beaming mommy as the centre of attention light a spark in your mind. All those years until then, you had been brushing away any broody ideas that ever cropped in your head—thinking you still wanted to work on that promotion, bungee jump in New Zealand, finish the list of hundred books you always wanted to read, learn to make chocolate and post pictures from all seven continents on your Facebook page—before you entered the no-exit world of parenting.

But you are somehow unable to ignore those ideas anymore. Suddenly, everyone around you is pregnant. The long lost friend from college you borrowed jeans from, calls to tell you that she is expecting a baby in three months; and so is your aunt's daughter. Your biological clock is ticking and there would never be the 'right' time to do this, you tell yourself. Not to mention, that the whole world around you is expecting you to multiply, and really quickly at that. You need something to look forward to every day, you need a new activity to do, new things to shop, a new place to visit, a new person to come home to. So having a baby seems like that foreign country you visit for an unprecedented experience or like that exciting start-up venture you own and grow with your responsible hands as against your very predictable and mundane daily job.

And one fine day you take the plunge. And how!

Never has peeing been as thrilling as it is now, with the pregnancy test stick in your hand. The two pink lines that flash on the stick are going to change your life forever.

Congratulations, you are pregnant! Shout-from-the-rooftops PREGNANT!

You don't have the slightest idea what you have signed up for. Ready or not, the baby is coming.

I hit a similar point about three and a half years into our marriage. I have always liked the idea of having kids, so I knew I would have at least one at some point in time. That I would actually start getting dreams about being a mother, was something I had never thought would happen. Cheesy as it may sound, I think motherhood really called me. Although we had started to plan a baby, I never expected to get pregnant this quickly—within a month. This was probably the fastest thing that I had ever done, except, perhaps, for a slow-cycling race at school where I had lost for riding the cycle faster than everyone else.

I found out about my pregnancy while holidaying in the US, at my sister's place. We had gone to a Mexican restaurant for lunch and a certain aroma put me off so much that my husband and I had to walk out without eating anything. We went to a mall later, and I was alternately feeling either extremely cold or extremely hot and sweaty every 15 minutes. The moment I'd bought an XL size frozen yogurt cup, I felt like having a hot steaming coffee, and right after I was done with the coffee I wanted to drown myself in a tub of ice cubes.

On our way back from the mall, we stopped at a pharmacy to buy pregnancy test kits. I bought two, just in case I didn't believe one and wanted to double check. Surely, I couldn't already be pregnant? Of course I had decided that I wanted to have a baby, but this was similar to deciding to bet all your money impulsively in one shot at the roulette table. The idea of taking a plunge gives you such a high, that sometimes you forget that the plunge is actually going to land you at an altogether different place from where you had jumped—a place from where you may never be able to go back.

I am not sure if there were the usual butterflies flitting away in my stomach or pregnancy was acting up, but my stomach felt really odd and my heart was almost in my throat. I was wearing a bluish-green sweatshirt that day that I can't even bother to look at now. I associate that colour with being pregnant and feeling queasy. No wonder the curtains in many hospitals are made in that colour; the colour has vomit written all over it. Writing about it, even now, makes me feel weird. It is the same with red onions that I ate that day. I can never eat those again in my life. They still make me nauseous.

So, this was it, I was going to take the test.

5 minutes later I came out of the bathroom, crying.

'Yes, the test is positive,' I told my husband.

'What is there to cry about, then?' he asked.

We hugged each other.

I was crying out of happiness, excitement, achievement

and surprise. But most importantly, I was crying out of the guilt of having had tequila shots at a friend's Christmas party about two weeks before.

Damn, I have wrecked my baby. I am possibly the worst mother and the worst woman on the face of this planet.

Apparently, the moment a man's sperm attaches to a woman's egg to create a baby; it also injects a lifetime's supply of guilt into her system—one that haunts her at every step of motherhood. Right from feeding formula to your baby, to dropping him at a daycare to join work and to accidentally throwing away one of his twenty-six ninja warrior toys—mommy-guilt stays with you until…well until you are a mommy.

So I did what any 21st century pregnant woman worth her salt would do to appease herself when faced with traumatic situations like the one I was in.

I Googled.

My dear friends—'Baby Center', 'What to Expect' and a million other pregnancy forums full of unknown expectant women—came to my rescue. My sister had a copy of the hard bound *What to Expect When You Are Expecting* from her pregnancy days. There was an entire section devoted to people like me, who had unknowingly had a little to drink during what possibly were the first few days of their pregnancies. It did not do any harm, said the book, since you didn't even know when exactly you got pregnant. Even if there was an embryo inside by then, it was too tiny to get under the influence.

The book also said that right from calculating my due date to actually bringing the baby home, it had everything figured out for me in its thirty-two odd chapters. The book was pregnant with information on what happens inside your body during pregnancy and how a foetus grows, complete with tips and tricks. I spent the next nine months cramming the book, learning from it how my son was growing from a peanut to a peach to a butternut squash, and balancing it on my belly in the last trimester. I must have thought that the mere physical proximity of the gospel to the site of action could work more in my favour.

It would be wrong to say that I had a tough pregnancy. I mean, there was the usual discomfort that everyone has to go through and the twenty-eight extra kilos I added to my body in the name of feeding the baby well. But other than that it went pretty okay. I had become very broody during my pregnancy—from decorating the baby nursery all on my own, to rearranging all cupboards, giving myself facial treatments and ironing baby burp cloths purchased well in advance—I did everything that was originally very unlike of me.

I was ravenously hungry all the time right from day one, despite feeling bilious. So I used to stock my bedside drawers with paneer paranthas to satisfy my 2 a.m. hunger pangs and gorge on an entire box of mangoes on a summer day. If you ask my husband, whose only frame of reference is Hollywood movies where pregnant women are shown hugging the toilet every morning with their hormones going wild, he will definitely say that I got a good deal. He wouldn't know much anyway, since he was away half the time in day long cricket matches, when poor, fat bellied me had to go maternity clothes shopping with his credit card, all by myself.

Can you imagine? All that my husband did to support me was to drive me to work and back every morning, getting late for work himself, bring me whatever I wanted to eat whenever I wanted, soak my feet in a hot water bucket in the evenings, be there for every single check-up appointment, and make sure I slept well.

While I was absolutely in love with my pregnancy—with my belly growing to be like my very own Lamborghini that drew attention from everyone around me—there were days when I wished for my husband to take the pregnancy over from me, like, give me weekends off or something. Or for me to go back in time to stop Eve from making Adam eat that goddamn apple. Or simply, for my husband and I to be born as sea horses—as, with them it is the male who carries the baby. (Additionally, the sea horses get to live in the sea, which is nothing short of heavenly for a woman who is heavily pregnant during summer and is sweating for twenty. Getting in and out of bathtub for her is the equivalent of running a triathlon with your body hanging upside down.)

Right after our wedding, Husband and I had moved from India to Singapore for our work. A couple of years after that, Husband was offered a job in Hong Kong and he was able to convince me to move again. And yet another year later, we moved lock, stock and barrel to Amsterdam. We were a carefree DINK (Double Income No Kids) couple back then, in those pre-baby days of the yore. We could just pack our bags and set sail. We never bought any real furniture or anything that couldn't fit into a suitcase. So we were never sure if we were going to stick in Amsterdam as well for this long, long enough to get pregnant and raise a child.

The child birth system in Amsterdam is a bit different from what I had seen or heard of in India, to say the least. My doctor here didn't see the need to confirm my pregnancy through any test. Although he did calculate the due date of my baby through a very state-of-the-art gadget—a small cardboard that was cut in a circle and had dates printed on it. By moving another smaller cardboard circle on top of that, he calculated and told me the date on which my baby would be born. Later on, he handed me a letter for a midwife and informed that doctors are not really involved in pregnancy and birth here, until and unless really required.

I could have run away from there right then, but something told me I should stick on.

We could even opt to have the birth at our home, like what one third of the local people here did, absolutely safely! But I was too chicken to try it, however exotic it may have sounded. It took us a few months to get to terms with the highly relaxed healthcare system here. Back in India, I was a person who would buy antibiotics like chewing gum and suspect a doctor if he didn't prescribe a laundry list of medicines for a case of eye twitching. But here, they lay stress on going as natural as you could, regardless of how much I craved for a pint of amoxicillin served neat to tame my sore throat.

The midwives were highly qualified and still did all the regular check-ups and ultrasounds. But at every check-up we met a different one, and who would eventually be there on the D-day was anybody's guess. We couldn't book a hospital in advance here; we could only give our preference for one. Only when the labour started, would the midwife call the hospital to check if there was space available for us and involve a doctor if some medical intervention was required. If the hospital was full, she'd take us to another one. I wondered how there were no cases of babies being born in the back seat of the car when trying to get to one hospital from the other, but I was told that somehow all of this always worked out. First baby, new country—this was going to be exciting *and* terrifying. So, both my parents had flown over from India to be with me for the delivery.

The due date came and passed. No baby. My mother-in-law in India called me and said that I shouldn't worry—since, according to her indigenous calculations, my due date should be three days after the one my doctor had told and the midwives had confirmed after a series of ultrasounds and other highly advanced tests.

Three more days passed, still no baby. My mother was loading me up on sesame seeds, nuts and other 'heat-inducing' foods. According to the highly advanced research centre of Old Wives, backed completely by unverifiable hearsay passed over from one generation to the other, such food when eaten during the last month of pregnancy make the baby feel hot and eager to come out. This is also the very reason why these foods are not allowed during the first months of pregnancy, so that the baby feels cold and stays inside. Now, you might think that hearing such things would annoy the hell out of a modern day pregnant woman. But you see, by the end of nine months we are completely maxed out on the whole world prying on our lives and giving us advice, so we don't really bother anymore.

I went out for dinner with my work colleagues and I was asked by someone if I was having twins, for I was as big as a duplex house, garage included (although, he didn't dare to utter that last part of the sentence).

'No, I am not,' I replied to him politely.

'Are you sure about that?' the cheeky sod felt the need to inquire further.

It would have been fine if his tone had a little taunt in it. But he genuinely thought I could have miscounted the number of foetuses inside me, and that it was his moral responsibility to remind me to make sure I didn't leave the hospital with lesser number of babies than I was entitled to.

'Oh, now that you say, maybe I should double check. Wait, how many children have you fathered? Zero, right?' came from my mental word processor that was permanently set to sarcasm font.

So now I was not only a sixteen-million-weeks-pregnant woman at work who would just not start her maternity leave, I was also as-huge-as-a-whale pregnant woman at work who got offended easily by non-parent idiots asking me what they thought were innocent questions.

But secretly I did think, 'What if there *was* more than one that the midwives had somehow failed to catch? Perhaps there were three in there, or eight! How scary and record-settingly incredible would that be?' The pregnancy was taking a toll on my brain and the heartburn, summer heat, sleeplessness and endless wait were slowly killing me. At one point I may have said, 'All right that's it; the show is over.

Let's go back to being *unpregnant* now.' I had been doing this pregnancy right all this while, doing exactly what the book had advised. And therefore I felt betrayed by my unborn child—to whom I had been providing 24x7 room service for the past forty weeks and over—for not showing up on time.

'Why, just why wouldn't he come out? Those are your genes coming to play there,' I told my husband, who is always late in reaching everywhere. He arrived late by a full two hours on our wedding day, when almost all the guests from my side had left.

Twice the midwives did a membrane sweep on me to kick-start labour, but this one was a strong-willed baby who couldn't be hurried up. (He continues to show those traits even now at the age of two; so basically, whatever nurturing I have done so far has had little or no effect on shaping his natural personality. I should probably just stop bothering with it at all now.)

Forty-one weeks up. Intervention could be discussed, they said. But I refused this time. I too wanted to do everything naturally, with hypnobirthing and the full shebang. (That I caved in for an epidural later was another story.)

By now every other woman I knew was having a baby, even the ones who were not pregnant. Or at least that's what I felt. My cousin was due to deliver three weeks after me and her son was born almost a month before mine. I was like that child whose parents are the last ones to pick her up from school—doubtful and dejected. I absolutely longed to get on the hospital bed and have the damn machines attached to my belly. In desperation, I even went to the hospital three times on account of false labour, only to be asked to wait longer. I even faked false labour once—yeah, beat me to that—just so I could see some action, as I was pretty sure there was no baby coming out of me.

Well, the silver lining of it all was that at least we were saved of the stress of finding an available hospital at the time of actual labour; as I was now a frequent visitor at this one, they were obligated to keep a spot for me. They should have given me a membership card to scratch and win points every time I went there. Besides, my case was not normal anymore and hence it was out of the hands of midwives.

My friend's gynaecologist mother in India made fun of me by saying that I was probably making an absolute genius inside that it was taking me so much time, and that she would have never waited that long if I were her patient. Every morning my mother would shower and get ready with the hospital bag to see me off; thinking today would be *the* day. But, by evening both of us would be killing time with yet another failed baking experiment subsequently used to feed pigeons in our balcony.

Six more days gone. They wouldn't let me go beyond forty-two weeks. So this was going to be my last night before I got induced to somehow get the baby out. I downed a full pineapple and a generous serving of extra spicy Thai green curry, as advised by the midwives, to induce labour naturally. They didn't prescribe these methods officially, as these were not based on any research. But I was willing to try out anything at that time. Another trick I had read that could do the job was to dance naked outdoors on a full-moon night. I tried that too partially, by exposing my belly as I slept, with a full moon coincidentally shining through my window that night. I had done that every night anyway during my last trimester, as I had a terrible itch on my belly that I could not scratch away.

Now, what business did the baby have to act on the outer surface of the stomach? Was it not enough that it was already creating havoc inside, colonizing all the space that was in there, all the way from oesophagus down to the cervix?

Right when they are in the womb, children learn to claim exponentially more territory than what is proportional to their pocket-size bodies. When they are introduced to a bed, they sleep with arms stretched out as if they are giving chest measurements for their rompers to a tailor and legs as if they are playing hopscotch.

In a way, pregnancy is very similar to raising a small child. Both keep you up all night, both make sure you are never alone, both keep the child at the forefront of your life—one literally and the other figuratively, both shrink your brain, expand your heart and make your sense of smell more pronounced than ever before—from 'those are definitely red onions frying in the neighbour's kitchen in the next street and I CAN'T stand the smell,' to 'there is something going on in that baby's diaper right now, that I can tell even from this side of the football field.'

I am not sure which one of those labour-inducing tricks worked, if at all they did. But I did wake up with cramps in my back at 4 a.m., about five hours before I was scheduled to go to the hospital anyway.

Stork Brings the Baby. Well, Not Exactly

So I did not have any dramatic water breaking or rushing to the hospital at the last minute and getting stuck in the traffic jam kind of deliveries that we see in the movies. We went to the hospital according to the appointment given to us, at 9 in the morning on a Saturday.

'Go on, say it. I know what you are thinking,' I teased my husband as we were getting ready to leave.

'What?'

'The hospital is making you miss your weekend cricket game today.'

'Not just a game. A real match. That too finals!'

'I can imagine what you might be going through. I wish I could take your pain, since I *really* don't have any right now.'

'Oh, don't worry. The game doesn't start until 11. I am sure we will be back before then.'

'Are you kidding me?' my eyes almost bulged out of their sockets.

'Why? Aren't you happy that I planned it so well? See, if I don't practice, how will I teach our kids?'

'Kids? Plural? Can we just handle this one for now? And why do they have to learn what you like?'

'They don't have to, but they will. I know.'

'Arghhhh. I don't have the patience to deal with this right now. I will hire a taxi and go. We will inform you when we are done and the baby is ready to come with you on the field.'

'Ha ha ha. Of course I was kidding and you were the one who started it, remember? I wouldn't miss being with the baby for the world. Baby first, sports later.'

'And wife?'

'Oh yes, her too. First, first. And I won't pressurize our kids into doing anything,' he paused for a bit and then teased me back with, 'as long as they turn out to be world class sports players when they grow up.'

'Glad we got that all "sorted".'

'Anytime, babes. Shall we go now?'

So the fourth time when we went to the hospital, we really thought this was it. I was already getting mild contractions in my back for the last few hours, so there was no doubt that the baby express had started from terminal uterus. We went all prepared with a bag full of four different baby outfits complete from head to toe *(since the baby couldn't appear in public wearing the same clothes every four hours)*, six pairs of underwear for me *(since we might just have needed to camp there for a week and our house was a full 10-minute-drive away)*, three change of clothes for me *(since my belly would have obviously shrunk back once the baby came out, so I couldn't decide which ones would fit)*, extra warm socks, leggings and hat for me *(since it was the 1st of September and temperatures might plummet from 20 to 0 overnight)*, lots of stuff to eat *(since the hospital might just starve us to death for having them work on a weekend)*, a pack of cards *(since it might be a good idea to shout 'I got a royal flush here' while breathing through contractions)* and a portable CD player. The husband came in his ubiquitous black Adidas track pants, which I sometimes think that he was born wearing. The label on those pants very clearly says, 'the brand with three stripes', just so that no one has any confusion whatsoever. Thank god for little mercies like lucidly explained clothing. Life with labour pains is tough enough.

The CD player that we carried was to play my hypnobirthing CD, which would put me in trance and make my mind totally aware of the entire baby delivering business while magically ignoring the pain associated with it. In a Zen-like fashion. The hypnobirthing book was another one that I had read over and over again during my pregnancy, which came along with this CD to train me on meditation during labour and delivery to manage pain.

Every night when I played the CD on to practice, a woman's balmy voice would ask me to relax each of my body part, starting from my head. I think this was the same woman who does the Siri voiceover in iPhones and can never understand my Indian accent. Each night I kept a target to finish the entire CD, but just as I got beyond relaxing my nose, I would start snoring with the earphones still intact in my ears.

On the day of my labour, I felt like that student who, a night before her exam, dozes off for a little bit to be fresh for a whole night of study, only to wake up 15 minutes before the actual exam, wondering what to do now. I somehow hoped that the CD would help me sail through the labour exam since I hadn't been able to study at all beforehand.

And to be fair, my head and nose *were* actually very relaxed during the labour, thanks to months of practising.

We reached the hospital and I was put on my dream hospital bed for a check-up. 20 minutes later a rather ruthless nurse announced that, lo and behold, those contractions that had been killing my back all these hours were still not real and hence the labour had not actually started. I couldn't believe my ears. I really tried to negotiate hard with the nurses, but they wouldn't have any of it.

'The contraction monitoring machine is showing only 45,' the nurse told me in a matter-of-fact manner, like I was too plebeian for her—just another woman having just another baby.

'So what is the cut off you need here?' I asked her helplessly, like a student who had flunked her exam.

'What is the "what" you need here?'

'Sorry, I meant how much does it have to be for actual labour?'

'At least a 100,' she replied in a very strict headmasterly fashion.

I hated biology in school, and now biology was starting to hate me. I was sent home yet again what with my bags and all paraphernalia to come back the same evening at 8. The entire day I kept feeling sporadic, painful cramps in my back, as if someone was hitting me with my husband's cricket bat several times in a go, and stopping only to take rest before hitting me harder.

'Surely, this can't be just 45 now,' I thought. 'What else did I have to bear to go over a hundred; be bitten by a blasted platypus?'

We went back at 7, just to not be late and miss out on the baby coming out, as I couldn't take any chances now. We wanted the best seats available for the show. I lay on the same bed again with all machines attached to me, and my husband's eyes glued to the contraction machine as if he was watching the World Cup finals.

Reams of graph paper kept coming out with haphazard lines peaking to a maximum of 60 and down again. All of a sudden, I screamed some expletives. Wowza! What the hell just happened? I was now almost lifeless and whimpering in pain, calling out for my mother, swallowing the last bits of pride I had. It was that bad. Hubby turned to me a couple of minutes later and tried to high five.

'You know what, we just crossed 130!' he said, with a spark in his eyes and a grin on his face.

I stared at him for a second before I exploded.

'It is not your Brett Lee making a century here. It is your wife dying away from labour pain and I could deal with a little less excitement right now!'

'Oh okay, I'm sorry,' and he sat down quietly.

'What now?' I asked him, after a few seconds of silence in the room.

'You said Brett Lee? Seriously? He is not even Indian! Or a batsman!'

'I know! But I don't care, all right?'

'You could have simply said Sachin Tendulkar, you know. It would have made more sense,' he replied in a mellowed voice, as if he was heartbroken.

'Do you think anything is making sense right now?'

It happened over and over again, and every time I felt as if someone had forcibly sent me on a giant wheel in an amusement park where I was crying for the ride to stop but it took me up again. My teeth were clattering and my entire body was shivering.

'No, it isn't cold in the hospital room. Shivering is normal in labour,' the nurse told us, who had probably been yawning all this while as I doled out sopranos from my mouth.

'Should I take the CD out?' Hubby asked.

I don't remember what I replied to that, but it definitely wasn't anything polite. It was all back labour for me and the pain was horrible, to say the least. I had only read that back labour is worse than regular labour. I hadn't experienced the latter so I can't judge. But I felt like a Lilliputian getting a lower back tattoo of the size originally meant for Gulliver, while going through the compounded period and constipation pain of my entire tribe. My mind had stopped working so I could not recall any of those breathing techniques that I had read about. The moment I'd start to think about how to deal with the pain, I was hit by another contraction.

Many hours of agony later, we asked the doctors about epidural and they said that they would need to phone the anaesthetist who might have just called it a day. They'd call her only if we were very sure of taking it.

'I think you should get the epidural,' Hubby said to me.

'B...but I had always wanted to do everything naturally!'

'It is still natural. You are not getting induced. All you are going to do is to manage that pain better.'

'Yes, but that takes away the thrill from it.'

'Listen, there is no need to be macho and bear all that pain. You are not here to prove anything to anyone. If technology exists, use it,' and he turned back to his phone.

'Epidural isn't exactly technology. You mean adva...hang on, another contraction, phoo phoo phoo phoooooooo... what the...okay, it's gone. You mean advancement in medical science.'

'*Potato potahto*. It's amazing how you can be a stickler for semantics even during your labour pains. Anyway, who is going to remember how you delivered? Not even you, yourself. It's not like they will etch the names of women who didn't use any drugs on their hospital roll of honour.'

'They won't, right?'

And that was all it took a strong willed, obsessed with natural birth, hypnobirthing-book-reading-me to say, 'Yes, I do want the epidural.'

They changed me into hospital scrubs and poked my spine with what felt like a parrying dagger. About 30 minutes later I could not feel anything down my lower body, and no pain or shivering whatsoever.

'Ha! Now bring on those contractions I say, I got my back covered,' quite literally at that.

I felt like a queen perched on the top of an ivory tower, being served with food and drinks, not lifting a finger to even visit the bathroom, while my baby slid down the birth canal at his own will. Hubby on the other hand was given a wooden chair to spend the night on—poetic justice I guess.

Watching contractions spiking on the graph but not feeling anything in your body was like enjoying a ferocious street fight from inside your double glass window house. The drug then started to act and my eyes felt heavy. I strongly believe that they should start marketing epidurals in the league of sauna treatments or marijuana—they are that relaxing. Around an hour later, I shut my eyes and drifted to wonderland.

Yes, I slept during my labour and had to be woken up every now and then by the doctors to check how I was progressing. GO ON AND JUDGE ME IF YOU HAVE TO! (LIKE I HAVE, A MILLION TIMES SINCE THAT DAY FOR TAKING THE EPIDURAL!)

At some wee hour in the morning, I was told that I had dilated enough to start pushing.

'Damn, the party's over,' I thought.

'It is just 4 a.m., could you let me sleep a little more so that I wake up fresh, brush, have breakfast and be ready for action?' I wanted to say to them, but thankfully I was not zonked that much to twaddle like that.

So they ruthlessly just shut the epidural off.

Holy Moly! Did that hurt or what? I was back to forced-on-a-giant-wheel helpless with cricket bats hitting my back harder than ever before, and had the often heard 'I can't do this, get the baby out another way' drama sprinkled all over.

'Don't give up. It's happening. I can see the baby's head. Come on, you can do it!' This was husband-talk for 'stop being such a baby'.

'You said that an hour ago! Stop lying to me and go ask the doctor to operate on me!'

'Your baby has a lot of hair! Curly hair!' one of the nurses exclaimed.

'God, I can't do thi...hang on...did you say curly? NONE OF US HAVE CURLY HAIR, HOW CAN THE BABY HAVE CURLY HAIR?' I shouted at the poor nurse as if it was her fault.

'Your sister has curly hair, doesn't she?' Husband tried to placate me.

'Wavy...ouchhhhh...not curly...phoo phooo. Are you checking the right baby here, nurse?'

'Go, go, go!' everyone ignored me and continued with their cheering.

At one moment, I felt a warm gush of something going out of my body.

'Look, what we have here!' the doctor announced gleefully.

'What? The baby's here? Okay, that's good, but do you promise me I don't have to do anything else now?' I had thought my tribulation would never end.

So almost 27 hours since the first cramp, a harried dad,

a war wrecked soldier of a mom and excessive body fluids later, our son was born. If I now look at him, it is hard to imagine that those twinkling eyes and chubby cheeks came into being through such a gruesome parturition process. You would think that something as magical as creating life should have a backdrop of rainbows, flowers, lush greenery and chirpy birds. Nada. There is blood, grime, placenta and a heavily sweating woman screaming like a banshee.

At the end of it all, I just wanted to turn to my husband and say, 'You know what, that *really* hurt and I am a bloody hero to have done that. I have created life from scratch. So honour me with a Nobel Prize here, dear Hubby, and never ever tell me how your neck hurts from using a wrong pillow at night. Henceforth, the pain bar has been set way too high for you to ever reach.'

But of course, you don't get a chance to say that (and never in your life will you get to say it to get anything done in your favour), since the attention of the whole cosmos has now shifted to your baby.

The umbilical cord was cut by Husband and my son was put on my chest for the first real skin-to-skin contact. That feeling, dear readers, is beyond words. So I shall not even attempt to describe it. Go have a baby just for that.

I couldn't believe that I was done after almost ten months of being pregnant, which felt like a lifetime. The feeling took some time sinking in. I touched my belly and saw that it had turned from a taut, huge igloo to a squishy, deflated tent with no one kicking and punching it from the inside. The inmate of that igloo was out in the world that I had to share him with. It was not only I who could touch, feel and communicate with him now. His new world was much bigger than my womb.

He was no longer just anticipation, no longer a part of my body, no longer a monochromatic photo and no longer an exotic fruit as per *What to Expect When You are Expecting* milestones. He was a real person with hands, toes, facial expressions and my husband's big nose—the one gene I had hoped my husband would forget to pack when sending his sperm away on a trip to my abode. And he was perfect!

My son's life wouldn't be measured in weeks now, but in months and soon, in years. His existence no longer depended on me, although mine still depends on him.

But phew, I really *was* done.

Get me a double cheese burger with extra fries and a large shake, and turn the lights off. I am going to sleep for three days straight, I wanted to say. And the world would laugh at me. The real work started now, I was told.

I indeed had no idea what I had signed up for. Even after supposedly preparing for all these months, I was so not ready for this. One can never be. No one is born a parent, the child makes you one—whether you turn out to be a good or a bad one is up to you.

My son was here: crying, hungry and tiny. And I was there: knackered, messy and unable to pee on my own.

Two years later: I am still knackered, only slightly less messy and still not able to pee on my own.

(Since my son now follows me to the bathroom.)

So This Is What It Looks Like

The hospital had a policy of discharging everyone the same day of delivery if everything went fine. While everything did go fine, they asked me and the baby to stay under observation for one more night as the pregnancy had gone beyond forty weeks.

So after I had showered, I was transferred to another room. The baby was wrapped up from head to toe and put in a see through plastic bassinet that was wheeled into this new room as well. The nurse told me that if I had any difficulty in peeing, I had to inform her and she would then attach a catheter inside me. I did not know what a catheter was and how it looked like. So I assumed it was definitely something bad. Nothing good can come out of the hospital with a name like that anyway. For a few hours I kept drinking water but had no urge to pee. After about four litres, I figured something was wrong.

I turned to Husband who was busy entertaining the

baby with his extempore rendition of spoken word poetry.

Easy baby, easy easy
Easy peasy Japanesee
Uncle Sam went to buy Chinesee
Papa getting sneazy sneazy…

When I interrupted with, '*Mama feeling uneasy uneasy*. Can you take me to the bathroom?'
'Sure.'
'Turns out I don't have to pee. Can you help me back to the bed?'
'Sure.'
'I think I do want to go now. Can you take me again?'
'Sure.'
'Not happening. Help me back to the bed?'
'Sure.'
'This time it's for real.'
'Sure.'
'Nope, back again. It's like I have to but I am unable to.'
'Sure.'
'Listen, can you…'
'I am calling the nurse.'

The nurse came in hurriedly and exclaimed, widening her green eyes, 'Why didn't you call me before? You have completely messed everything up now!'

She inserted a tube in me, which had a container at its other end. And urine started to flow. It flowed and flowed until the container got full. They emptied it and brought a new one. Twice.

'Your wife, sir, will be a great mother. She has a massive control over her bladder. I think we emptied enough liquid from her to irrigate a paddy field,' the nurse told my husband in a rather congratulatory manner.

'Control over bladder = Great mother?' I wondered then. 'Hell, yeah,' I can say now.

You never know what fear can make you do. The fear of getting a catheter installed kept my body going on without peeing for hours, hoping all would be fine on its own eventually. A plastic bag was now put at the end of the tube that I had to carry with me everywhere I went. Then I realized that this was the exact same thing that geriatric patients used to carry with them.

All I needed now was to wear round golden rimmed spectacles, put crochet covers on my desktop computer and laugh with my fellow oldies at a yoga class in the park. Overnight I had turned from a pregnant woman into my great grandmother. And I absolutely hated it.

The night I stayed back, my husband or parents were not allowed to stay with me. The nurse offered to take my baby away for the night so that I could rest well. I may confess that I jumped at that offer, as much as I could with my sore limbs. Although at that time I did show some concern over strangers taking away my son for an entire night, even if to a room right next to the one I was in.

Now that we are on the topic of confessions, let me also add here that I did not instantly fall in love with my baby when I saw him for the first time like many people say they do. The love grew over days and months and I haven't experienced loving anyone that much ever. But it definitely wasn't instant. The love was also there when he was still inside me, but just that moment when I saw him first, I was a little bit more concerned about how he looked and if his hair was straight or curly as announced by the nurse when he had first crowned. I am a sucker for straight hair.

I know that sounds horrible, but I had a type for babies I liked. Although now I want to bear hug them all and take them to my house. (Except the ones with runny noses, since my own son's snot is enough for me to handle right now, what with him wiping his nose on my jeans multiple times a day.)

It takes you some time to adjust to the fact that your newborn doesn't look like the chubby bubbies you see in Pampers commercials. He may grow into one sooner than you can imagine. That is when you will feel that yours is the cutest baby that has ever been produced by mankind, period.

But right when he is born, he has a giant head full of cradle cap (which is something like sticky dandruff but a lot worse), fuzzy hair all over his body, an off-centre chin, a barely-there-neck (that a person who has never seen an infant up close will never remember to support), structurally unsound legs, a clamp supported belly button, and several bruises and blotches over his entire body. Of course he is still cute in his own vertically challenged sort of way and will get his due shares of likes and 'awws' on Facebook. But pretty much every baby gets that these days. So that isn't a fair evaluation at all.

Have you ever seen anyone comment on a newborn

baby's picture with, 'Oh, those eyes are really bulging out of that bald head, are you sure you want to keep him with you?' or with, 'I wish Facebook had an unlike button, as I really don't like that ugly baby of yours?'

Either it is customary to show appreciation for all babies publicly on an autopilot mode. Or that all babies in the world *are* indeed beautiful. The pre-baby me would have gone with the former view, but not anymore! How motherhood makes you a better person! I genuinely feel now that babies really are the best looking people around—all of them. Yes, even the ones with curly hair. Now whenever I see a baby, any baby, I can't help but feel that it looks like mine in one way or the other.

I was woken up at 7 in the morning with a tray of toasted bread, butter, jam, orange juice and a crying baby on the side.

'He needs his mama,' the nurse plonked the baby onto my arms and went to air out the room that smelled from my continuous sweating from the last night, despite it not being that warm.

That was my first experience of *Thou Shall Never Be Allowed to Eat in Peace* commandment of motherhood.

'Bu...But...I don't know what to do. This is my first time. Can you send someone to help?' I almost pleaded to the nurse.

'You are a smart, grown up woman. Of course you can handle him,' and she walked out of the room.

'Yeah, right. Can't take a side on my own to save my life, and I can take care of my baby. What do these people think?' I muttered to myself.

I immediately made an SOS call to the husband who was snoring away at home.

'Come quickly and get us. I can't move, and now I have a baby on top of me,' I tried to make it as dramatic as possible.

'Eh?' Husband's standard retort to my panic calls.

'Remember, we have a B-A-B-Y now?' I was pretty sure that in his half-awake state he had a hard time recalling what all had construed on the previous day.

'Of course.'

'Remember, he is still in the hospital with me?'

'Of course.'

'Remember, how you went back home last night and had to leave me all alone here?'

'Oh, stop rambling now. What happened?'

'You really don't know what I am getting at? COME NOW, I CAN'T DO THIS ON MY OWN,' I screamed into the phone.

'Call the nurse to help you.'

'I did, but the nurses are now busy with new pregnant women and won't help me. Those ditchers have other fish to fry now. Can you imagine?'

He reached about an hour later. We packed everything up and I was taken to the car on a wheelchair that had a 'It's a boy!' helium balloon tied to it, to let everyone know what we had achieved. On my way outside I had a strong urge to blow air kisses and wave at everyone around, just like an Olympics winner would do on his home return while showing off his winning trophy. But to my utter dismay, no one in the hospital seemed to care for anything other than their own sickness. What a bunch of egotistical people we have living around us! There was no one whistling and clapping for me there. For them it was yet another addition to the seven billion population of the world.

But for me it was *the* entire world.

Hubby had duly pasted a 'Baby on board' yellow sticker at the back of our car, which, to be honest, was more to display our pride than to signal to fellow automobile drivers to drive carefully around us (nobody around you really cares about that sticker and the message you are trying to send with that). And all four of us—the baby, my husband, me and my catheter—sat in the car and drove home where my parents were waiting for us with balloons and all that jazz.

So we were back from what felt like a really long and painful grocery shopping trip. Except, this grocery shopping trip had changed my life forever. And how! I had returned home as a mother. A MOTHER! I would now be filling administrative forms for someone where I would write my name under the 'mother's name' textbox.

The first days of postpartum are such a blur. You haven't even recovered from the whole delivery trauma and you have another life to tend to. You can't sit since your bottom hurts, you can't stand since your legs ache, and you can't sleep for long since you have to feed the baby every couple of hours. You can't even hold your own baby for more than a few minutes since your body feels like jelly. It feels like a truck just ran over you and left you almost lifeless. You dread your first postpartum bathroom visit like a first-time skydiver dreads taking a plunge into the air, since you don't know your body anymore. You feel like a science experiment gone wrong. Your baby is so fragile that you fear you might break it. You check on your baby every moment to make sure he is still breathing. Despite continued prodding by my mom, I refused to have my son sleep next to me since I feared I would roll over him and smother him.

Now there were things I knew would happen when I would have a baby. Friends and books had given me a rough idea of what to expect. I had heard from a lot of parents on how babies don't sleep in the nights, how they cry incessantly and how your life goes totally out of control. But honestly, somewhere deep down I thought that none of those messy things would happen with me or my awesome baby. Don't ask me why, but I just did.

In my mind was a picture of me ready to go for power yoga three days postpartum, a calm and relaxed baby giving me clear signals on what he wanted, my weight dropping like the jeans that were too loose on my waist and my life completely under control. (The people who tell you that this actually happened with them are lying. If they are not lying, then please congratulate them on their fake unicorn baby the next time you meet them.)

First-time parents live in a bubble. The one that is created by images of super slim mommies with shampooed hair, feeding their super happy babies with Avent milk bottles. Or by those of Hugh Grant of daddies waltzing away with their babies looking drop dead gorgeous at 2 a.m., in a clean house with all laundry folded and put away.

None of the advertisements for baby gear on the internet that we research for months have any *real* people in them. They never show a mother's nipples bleeding when she is using a breast pump. Never ever is a baby shown frowning, let alone crying. The mothers in those images seem to have a day comprising only of blowing bubbles in their babies' tummies and radiating trance level calmness all the time. Their eyes are devoid of any dark circles and their clothes freshly ironed and free from any spit or stains. They even have make-up on their faces. Make-up, ha! No, make that ha ha! And some more.

Let me tell you how I looked and how most of the moms look, not days, but months after the baby is there. (Unless of course they live in the Buckingham Palace, where an entire battalion is at their disposal to change one diaper.)

Wearing washed pajamas every day was the only standard I maintained. Coordinating their colours with tops would have been taking it a tad too far. Only the tops that fulfilled the functional ability to be quickly unfastened with one hand were considered—which were no more than three; so Thursday was not a good day for visitors, considering Sunday was the only laundry day.

My hair was still there on my head and that was all that mattered. While going out, I wore maternity jeans. Since the jeans didn't have the normal zipper or buttons, they were easy to pull up. Only once I didn't realize that I had pulled them up in the wrong direction—with back pockets now at the front—and found out after I was back home from my indulging hand sanitizer shopping trip, feeling something funny with my jeans all that while (I was simply happy with the luxury of being at the supermarket all by myself). And that was fine too.

Once it got cold, the only jacket I could fit in was my husband's huge downy black North Face coat, the sleeves of which covered my hands and made me look like an arctic fox. You see, I was sure I was going to lose that weight really quickly, so I didn't want to invest in any large-sized clothes for me at that time. Some may call that practical and economical thinking, I now call that 'who was I kidding'.

So that was my fashion statement as a new mom.

Don't even get me started on personal grooming, or the lack of it. It should suffice to say that once when Hubby was not in the house, I woke up from my nap and got dead scared to see a rather manly, hairy leg creeping out of my blanket—only to realize a few seconds later, that the leg was my own. That was the day when I decided I was going to invest time in myself, to look and feel good.

Hence, I ordered myself two new pairs of pajamas that wouldn't roll up my legs easily and show the foot-long hair when I slept.

But the thing is that if there is a time in a woman's life when her own looks don't matter to her at all, it is the time when she has just become a mother. Motherhood is so beautifully consuming that there is nothing else you want to do or be associated with. You'd rather spend time sterilizing your baby's bottles than getting your eyebrows plucked in those 15 spare minutes. The scruffy department was not entirely owned by me in our house, though. The first two weeks when Hubby was on leave, he too didn't get a chance to shave. Or maybe just had a valid excuse not to.

New parents are also extremely cautious and overly gullible. They will sell an arm and a leg to buy the very best, clinically proven, experts approved, BPA-free stuff for their babies. A few months later they either laugh at themselves or don't dare to admit to each other that the super expensive electric swing, for which they paid more custom duty than the actual price of the swing to import from another country, was used by their baby for a total of 6 minutes—including the time it took to set it up.

Once while still pregnant, Husband and I had gone for baby goods shopping. I had made a spreadsheet in advance that I took with me, which had all baby things to buy based on research on internet—complete with brands, names of shops to buy from and a status column against each to indicate the progress. So, while trying to pick a mattress for our son's cot from an array of mosquito free, air circulatory, soft, firm and perfect spine development enhancing mattresses, we asked a salesperson to help us decide on one. Now, he wasn't the one to mince words and he told us that any mattress other than the most expensive spine development one had a small risk of our baby dying. Dying he said. Of course we were going to pick the most expensive one, but why would the shop be allowed to stock all other varieties of murderous mattresses is still beyond me.

My son has mostly been a tummy sleeper, so the spine development aspect of that life sustaining mattress hasn't been of any use to us till date. Just like that swing imported from the US. Or those clips to fix the car seat on to the stroller. Or that Fisher Price sea horse that is supposed to help babies sleep. Or that blanket that can work both in summer and winter by adjusting the layers in it. Or that toy iPhone that looks just like the real one, but is still not the real one, Mama. Or that packet of fifty colourful plastic balls that guaranteed hours of fun. Or, check this out, *another* swing for toddlers we got our son for his first birthday on which only Miffy—the made in China musical stuffed rabbit that just would not stop singing—swings sometimes.

Or that baby book that I had bought when I was about five months pregnant and my son had kicked for the first time.

It seemed like quite a milestone then that needed to be celebrated with some online shopping, only for those kicks to turn into all night football practices a couple of months later. The book had pages to paste baby's pictures right from the ultrasound scans up until his first birthday. I haven't got the time to paste any yet. I may have some after my retirement but I will need to use that time to find that book first. The ultrasound scans are quite hazy to say the least, they look the same for all babies and, more often than not, you cannot make out head from toes. People have started posting those to their Facebook pages these days. What do they expect others to comment? 'Wow your blurry foetus has got your eyes!' or 'If this is what he looks like as a foetus, I can't even imagine how cute he looked as a spermatozoon. Do you have those pictures to share too?'

I did start filling in the first few pages of that baby book with names, birth dates and other such details of both me and my husband in the book, going as far as filling all of that for our extended families, hoping that somewhere at some point this exercise would make sense. Next was the section that asked for dates from when the baby first rolled over, first smiled, first burped, got his first tooth et al. Now I don't remember all of that, and I don't see the need to. It is not like we are going to celebrate his burp anniversary every year with aerated drinks served on the house. The first time he got his tooth was the time he stopped eating for hours and cried till it made his voice hoarse. No thank you, I don't want to remember that, I'm just happy he got his teeth. It feels quite creepy to preserve his first lock of hair in that book. I don't need to record his monthly height and weight in there too, as I don't have to pack him and ship him somewhere.

And hence, that baby book also lies buried under cobwebs in some corner of the house along with all the other useless stuff that I had bought.

If we add up the costs of all things new parents buy and never use in a year, I am pretty sure we will get to a figure that is close to the GDP of Zimbabwe. God, that hedonistic thought just makes me want to drown myself in my baby's spit.

My dear unborn, undecided, un-conceived, unplanned, un-discussed-with-my-husband second child,

If you do wish to surface on this earth one day, you will be given all that to use that your brother did not.

We are not going to buy anything new for you. We are wise enough now to know that a baby wipe warmer that electrically warms up wipes to the right temperature is really not a necessity, since those wipes are not ice cold to start with. And the steamer that has to be kept miles away from you so you don't touch it, does nothing to alleviate your cold.

Of course we will love you both equally, but will love you a teeny bit more if you really like that electric swing.

Will you?

Love,
Mama

Wait a second. I feel terrible now for saying those things. What kind of a mother would talk like that to their children? No, stop! Don't take me on a guilt trip here. I may have to come around on whatever I just said. I can't believe I am falling for this even before you are conceived!

Breakfast (and Lunch and Dinner) of Champions

A couple of weeks passed and my son was now getting into a routine of nursing every two hours on the dot. I was now free from that urinary catheter that I had to carry with me everywhere like a third arm. My body had started to heal and I was able to make sense of the world and tell day from night, when I got hit by mastitis. I was back to the bed again with high fever and ache and a dosage of pencil-sized antibiotics, which later on gave me thrush that lasted for two months. In case you are thinking that I have suddenly moved on to the topic of fauna variety found in the Amazon forest, let me tell you that mastitis and thrush are problems associated with nursing and pretty nasty ones at that.

No one, I repeat, no one ever tells you before what a big pain nursing is going to be. The images that conjure up in your mind when you think about nursing are those of a beatific Mother Mary feeding baby Jesus, emitting divine grace. It is just a baby who will suckle slowly with his tiny mouth, you think. How can it ever hurt? But dear Lord, it so does hurt. Yes, it is the best thing for your baby and for you, and the endorphins you release during it make the whole process worthwhile. But that does not take away the fact that it is one of the hardest things to do in the whole baby making course.

For starters, babies don't know that what they want is what their mothers are giving them. Those clueless little puppies! They just don't latch well enough to the breast, or latch too hard in a bout of extreme starvation causing pain and soreness. They need to be fed every couple of hours as their bodies can only take that much milk at a time, besides breast milk gets easily digested. My son used to take almost an hour for every meal, getting knocked out during the process. And when he finished, it was almost time for his next feed. So basically, I was providing him food round the clock. And then there was this constant anxiety of whether he got enough to drink, why is he still crying if he is full and oh my god, will he ever stop suckling so I can scratch my itching belly in peace.

I used to have disturbing dreams about that tiramisu I couldn't have due to its alcohol content for the whole year I was nursing and almost ten pregnant months before that. Those were some really difficult times! Even months after weaning the baby, I had to remind myself that it was okay to eat the 'prohibited food' now as there was no baby inside me or hanging on to me with his mouth open.

Engorgement, leaking, clogged ducts, baby biting you, being treated like a human pacifier, wrestling with that arduous contraption called the breast pump—the breastfeeding woes are endless. Many times in your tired state, especially during the nights, you forget the last time when you had nursed him. Now they do have apps for tracking all of that—complete with a stopwatch to track when your baby starts and stops his nursing session, even details like the last time he had a wee and a poo, his last nap etc., and graphs to analyse all that data. I downloaded one and used it a few times too. But it felt so awkward to do that. Baby is crying for milk, and you start the app and press keys to enter data? It is preposterous! I only had a tablet and not a smartphone then, which was difficult to manoeuvre with half a free hand, all right! (Of course it wasn't awkward to act like a nerdy parent at all. What were you even thinking?)

The pain from thrush was so bad that I would wake up crying in the middle of the night and felt needles poking into my chest after every time I nursed. Doctors advised me to stop nursing altogether since they were not able to fix my problem. But the guilt made me go on. I thought I'd be a horrible mother if I would not breastfeed my baby when I could. Even after all that struggle, there were evenings when my son would just not nurse, despite nursing fine the whole day, and wanted a peg of formula with water to sort of wind the day down in his own style. And that would really, really make me break down.

A new mother's mind is as fragile as a castle of cards. Touch it or as much as blow over it and it will collapse. Almost all new mothers will cry by the third or fourth day of postpartum, seemingly for no reason at all. Once your child leaves your body, he leaves a permanent hole in your heart, one that will fill up with tears at anything unpleasant that happens around you, only to be empty again. From hearing a stranger's baby crying in the supermarket to watching a C.R.Y. advert on TV asking for donations, you will well up at just about everything worth or not welling up for. You will suddenly start noticing that there is a lot that is wrong with the world that you have brought your child into—like hairy men zooming away on their bikes without silencers when you take your baby out or people smoking in public in the air that your child breathes, to say the least. The very fact that you can't fix any of that and that you will have to raise your child in a world full of evil, will make you feel even more sombre.

Every piece of bad news related to children that you hear will make you shudder at the thought that *that* could have been your baby and will make you hug them harder that day. The flight that just got crashed could have had *you* in it. You feel much more insecure than ever before even about your own life now, since it means so much more to someone else.

But there is nothing you can do about those tears. Birds fly, babies cry, and their moms cry too. Only dads have the sanity and strength to still stay chin up and walk ahead steering through this quagmire of hormones around them.

My husband was back to work after two weeks, and one afternoon I called him.

'Hey, what's up, are you busy?'

'Not really, tell me. All well? What is the baby doing?'
'He just slept.'
'So why don't you sleep too?'
'Yes, I was about to but I just couldn't.'
'You should rest as much as you can; he will be up in no time.'
'Yes, I know, but…'
'What?'
'He didn't drink that bottle I had worked so hard to pump.'
'It's okay; you can give it to him later.'
'No. I heated it up, so now I can't use it again.'
'So what's the problem? You can pump again right?'
'Yes, I guess.'
'Okay then, anything else?'
'Umm…no.' Sob sob sob, tear floodgates opened.
'What happened?' Hubby asked in an alarmed voice.
'He didn't even let me nurse him last evening.'
'So?'
'Why is he doing that to me?'
'What are you saying? He is a baby. He doesn't know what he is doing!'
'But why doesn't he understand that I am working so hard for him?' Sob sob sob sob.
'See you are making an issue out of nothing. He doesn't have anything against you. At least not yet.'
'What do you mean by "at least not yet"? What have I done? Do you even know how hard this mom business is? You are easily sipping away your coffee and chitchatting

with your colleagues at work. And here I am feeling like a total failure of a mom who can't even perform the basic task of feeding her baby well. It's like getting tired in the first 10 minutes of a marathon. How will I ever be able to face the bigger challenges in life if I can't handle this one now?'

'Slow down there. I was only joking.'

'Okay.' Sob sniff sob sniff sniff sniff.

'Listen, stop blaming yourself. It is not a big deal if he doesn't want to nurse at times. Don't you sometimes feel like ordering yourself a pizza and not eating home cooked food? Same is with him. He has his moods and tastes.'

'Yeah, right. Just two weeks old and he already has an awareness of his tastes and moods. What do you think he is?'

'Exactly my point. He is too little to understand a thing and you are judging yourself way too hard. You yourself said that you were going to give him formula once a day so that he stays used to it. So why are you stressing out now? Think about the women who are not able to lactate, are they not feeding their babies well?'

'Of course they are. I am not judging anyone here. Can you not be logical for once when we are discussing emotions?'

'Okay, so what really is the point? Why are you crying?'

'That ruthless man shot so many children in a school in the US. It was in the news. What wrong had those children done?'

'Yes, that is indeed sad. Let's talk about it later.'

'See, and you ask me why I am crying?'

'Okay, I need to run into a meeting now. You take care and sleep well. I will be home soon.'

'But what about the killings in Syria? Was it the fault of those poor families?'

'Bye.'

'These men are really heartless at times. Oh what's that? Baby's up, already? For how long was I on the phone?'

To my surprise, my son eventually did come around to nursing like a champ the day I stopped fussing about it. That is when I realized how stupid I had been to beat myself up like that, notwithstanding the fact that I had been trying beyond my best. I had this pressure on my head all the time to not lose the 'exclusively breastfed' badge and feed my baby something that was less than ideal. It is not as if the badge was going to be displayed on my epitaph or on my son's report card at school, or define how I had fared as a mother!

Parenting, I realized, is not a competition with your own self, and least of all with anyone else. It is completely personal and mostly banal. By adding our own challenges and ideals, we are just trying to infuse some excitement into it, which is really not required. We don't have to treat everything like a success or failure here, unlike our other fiercely competitive lives. You will always end up doing more than half of the things you thought you'd never do as a parent—letting kids play on your phone or giving them McDonalds's junk food for dinner because they won't eat anything else. And that does not make you any less of a parent.

Before I had my baby, I had this image in my head of not being 'that' mom. The one whose child lies down on the floor like a wet noodle in the supermarket throwing a tantrum for a candy and she just lets him be. Or the one who lets her child wear a Batman cape with Spiderman tights on a hot summer day as he just wouldn't wear anything else. But after I had my baby, I totally became 'that' mom. I now know that you can't even define a perfect parent, let alone be one. The fact that you strive to be better every day and allow yourself some harmless slack is good enough.

Before becoming a parent myself, I used to judge other parents. (I have judged my own too at times when I found fault with myself.) But now I empathize with them. If I walk past a mom or a dad whose child is not doing what he should be doing, I don't even stop to look and just go on with my business. And believe me, that is exactly what parents expect others to do. They are already stressed out and embarrassed enough to have some stranger curling their lip in disdain towards them and looking at their child with pitiful eyes.

It is easy to talk that wisely in retrospect now. But when my son and I were still new to this parenting–getting parented game, I blamed myself for everything that even bordered on going wrong with him. Once I couldn't figure out if he was hot or cold, because how was I supposed to? I assumed he was waking up in the night because of the chill and I put him in a very warm sleeping bag. The plan backfired as he woke up with rashes all over because of overheating. I must have berated myself a million times for that, until everything got fine—which was the very next day. When he got his first diaper rash, I put a little too much antiseptic cream on his bum that didn't come off the next day. I freaked out thinking that I have scarred my baby for life and lay awake almost the whole night waiting for it to be morning so I could call Sudocrem customer service. Another time, I accidentally flapped my hand on his cheek when he was wiggling too much. While I bawled like a baby for doing that, the actual baby in the house had a surprised look on his face, thinking, 'What the hell is wrong with her?'

There were times when I yelled out of helplessness just like there were times when I let him cry for a few minutes to take a breather. There were nights when I didn't change his diaper in the wee hours out of tiredness just like there were nights when I had that odd cup of coffee that supposedly contaminated the breastmilk and got him too excited to fall asleep. There was that split second when I turned my gaze away from him and he decided to dive from the bed and bruise his forehead, and there was that moment when I bumped his head into the wall when picking him up from his cot—oh how badly I wanted to go back in time to not let that happen! He has hurt himself at least a million times after that and it is no longer a big deal. He falls and I let him decide for himself first if it hurts or not. But, back then his pain looked like it could never get any worse or might never get any better.

All those times, I sulked more than my boy cried. I apologized to him more than he cared. I felt like a bad mommy more than I ever patted my own back. I might as well document all of the above in that baby book I had bought, instead of documenting his milestones.

And I should perhaps label all that under: 'Give yourself

a break, Mommy; you were quite an idiot thinking you'd get it right the first time'.

Maybe I should also document my own firsts as a mother there to congratulate myself on what all I *did* achieve. Achievements about the time when I tackled tough decisions like choosing between letting him eat the food he threw on the floor vs risking him getting impatient while I cooked again. Or the time when I drove for an hour and a half aimlessly in my night gown to make him fall asleep. Or the time when I cut and polished my toenails while still nursing him and talking on the phone.

There! That is quite a list of mommy milestones to feel chuffed about, isn't it? And here I was feeling bad about dropping mint sauce from my plate of pakoras on the head of a baby sleeping in my lap!*

---

*In my defence—I did not want to wake him up by removing him from my lap; I was very hungry and the mint sauce didn't have any spices in it.

Congratulations on Finishing Second in the Parenting Game. (So What If There Were Only Two Participants!)

'I love to hear babies cry!'—said no one ever.

If that crying baby is not your own or related to you in any way, his cries will sound more exasperating than heartbreaking to you. Hell, even a parent won't find those cries heartbreaking when they are sleep deprived and their kid is howling at 2 a.m. just because he is not being allowed to play his plastic piano. Remember that flight where the couple next to you had a baby who started screaming like a siren the moment the flight took off and did not stop until it landed? Remember how you shifted in your seat, gave dirty looks to that couple and suffocated yourself with a pillow? Remember when you updated your status on Facebook as: *Travelling with a crying baby next to me, god help me*; and thought to yourself, 'Why do people have children when they can't make them stop crying?'

Eat your words now, dear parent. You are that couple

and that flight is your life now. Every single day.

A baby's cry is not any normal cry that subsides after a few minutes. It is a cry that would put any supersonic jet to shame. A cry that would make even a trivial activity like bathing him seem like a torture from medieval times. Research suggests that hearing a baby cry can increase the blood pressure and heart rate levels of their mothers. I, for one, can definitely vouch for that. No other force in the world is powerful enough to interrupt your biological activities. A crawling cockroach or a sudden explosion in the house come close, but nothing else.

I shudder to think of those first days when my son cried so miserably with his eyes closed, face bloodshot and hands and feet in air coiling up like a spider. What could possibly be wrong with him? What sort of a mother was I if I didn't even know what upset him? Of course there was the usual reason of hunger, but what else? The poor thing couldn't even say if he was hot, cold, scared, uncomfortable, in pain, constipated or bored? Okay bored might be taking it a bit too far in terms of assessing a newborn baby's temperament. But otherwise, what is to tell you what's going on there? If only babies came with a user manual, life would have been much easier.

For the pint size that those babies have, it is unbelievable how they can scream at a pitch that can curdle their mothers' breast milk. But they do, and very helplessly, and somewhat nails on a chalkboard annoyingly at that. Now we didn't want to give our baby a pacifier, because I had read that it wasn't good for the baby in the long run. It made them hide their feelings which later developed into parafunctional activities like nervous nail biting when they grew up. I had read a bit too much about this parenting psychobabble, if you ask me.

Giving him some extra formula would almost always shut my son up. But you don't want to overfeed and have even bigger tummy problems late at night. That is the peculiar thing with babies. Whatever discomfort they have—gassiness, repulsion to a certain toy or general discontentment with life—they will always keep their feelings to themselves during the day and let it all out at the night. It is almost as if they punish us for inflicting something unwanted on them in their own evil way. That is not to say that they don't cry during the day, but they cry much more at night.

For us the 'witch hours' used to be between 10 p.m. and 2 a.m.—the prime time for resting for an adult body. Every night my son would sleep between 8 and 9, and so after dinner I used to retire to bed too. All seemed to be going well for a little while, when he would wake up screaming bloody murder, which then continued intermittently for a few hours. So we used to do the routine of—diaper check, hunger check, stomach cramps medicine check, lights on, lights off, music on, music off, pick him up, put him down, pick him up—and finally blame it on global warming or something such.

While surfing on the internet, I came across the *Dunstan Baby Language* which swears that there are only five reasons for which babies cry, and if we hear their cries closely, we can really make out what they want when.

So, it said that a cry that sounds like '*Neh*' means hungry,

'*Owh*' means tired, '*Eh*' means burp me, '*Eairh*' means gassy, and '*Heh*' means discomfort like the need of a fresh diaper. Ms Dunstan, who discovered this, has written books on this topic and has got a lot of acclaim. The trick she says is to listen carefully and spot those sounds really early when those babies just start voicing them, because in a few moments all of those sounds will turn into deafening *wah wahs* and you would be running from pillar to post figuring out what to do to calm them down.

'So that sounds easy,' I thought. 'My baby will be the happiest kid on the block now that I know this. So why do babies cry at all, now that we have discovered what they are crying for? This is the Holy Grail all harried parents have been looking for!'

I am not being sarcastic here and I don't doubt Ms Dunstan's research. I was with her until '*Neh*' and my son did make that sound when he was hungry. And then she lost me. How do you spot the difference between '*Eh*' and '*Heh*', eh? And that '*Heh*' that implies discomfort can mean a million things. Perhaps he didn't like the bed sheet colour that night, for all you know?

The following was a typical scene from a night at our house:

<*Baby starts to cry*>

'Baby is crying. I think he is hungry,' Husband calls me.

'But he just had his milk an hour ago. Did he say, "Neh"?'

'Yes, that's what he is saying,' he replied with a great level of self-assurance.

'That is not "Neh",' I retorted. 'If he is upset, it doesn't always mean that he is hungry. If it were that easy, no babies would ever cry, all books written about them would be torn to make paper boats and their poop would smell of roses. Since none of that happens, it means that we need to spend more time just observing our baby and registering his habits. We can then draw out patterns for better predictability...'

'Eh?'

'Why can't you ever understand what I am saying and always come back with a lame "eh"?' I asked him, getting irked.

'I wasn't listening to what you were saying. I was just thinking that if not "neh", his cries could be "eh"?'

'You weren't listening to me AGAIN?'

'Yes, because we were both trying to listen to the baby here, remember? No, that can't be "eh", since I already burped him,' once again he declared with confidence and an added sense of achievement.

(Burping was always Hubby's job. He could connect with that really well and this was one of the only baby care things that produced a result, and quite a vocal one. I could almost hear him say, 'That's my boy', when after a few manoeuvres, my son would let out a loud rumble.)

'Well he can't be tired, since he just woke up some time ago and his diaper is clean. So that leaves us with gas. Or perhaps he is too cold?' I thought aloud.

<Baby's cries have turned into loud wails>

'No, he's wearing so many layers. He can't be cold,' replied Hubby.

'Why have you wrapped him in so much? That is why he is crying! Let me take that blanket off. Look at yourself.

Are you wearing that many clothes?'

'What are you doing? He is a baby, he needs to wear more.'

'Says who?'

'Says common sense.'

'Of course he is hot. And that is why he is crying.'

'How do you know? You only said he could be gassy as well?'

'I know because I am his mom and I stay up all night with him.'

'You are not the only one who stays up awake with him.'

'Really? Do you come to nurse him at night?'

'If I could then I would. I do not doubt the hard work you put in even for a second. So you can also show me some appreciation every now and then.'

'Yeah, whatever.'

<Baby has completely gone bonkers>

'I am taking him to the living room with me', Hubby said determinedly.

'And stimulate him more with the TV, so he gets even more awake?'

'Is what you are doing helping him at all?'

'What do you mean by that? Today again you made that scratchy Velcro sound from the iPad cover. Didn't I tell you he gets scared by that?'

'I didn't do that intentionally; and stop making a fuss out of such a little thing. He has to learn to get used to everything.'

'You also made such a horrific sound when you kissed

him. I told you he doesn't like that.'

'He is my son too and I can do whatever I want.'

'No you can't. See he is crying even louder now. Can you just shut up and go away?'

'I think the sleeplessness has gone to your head. I am taking him away and we will talk once you are back to your senses.'

'Oh shut up. Just shut up,' that was the best I could come up with with a head full of rage.

<Slam! The door was shut>

'DON'T GIVE HIM THE COLIC DROPS JUST YET. THEY MAKE HIM REALLY DROWSY SO I WONDER WHAT THEY PUT IN THOSE. I DON'T THINK HE IS GASSY,' I screamed behind shut doors.

'I KNOW WHAT I AM DOING HERE. STOP GIVING ME INSTRUCTIONS FOR GOD'S SAKE,' he screamed back.

<Double Slam!>

Thanks, but no thanks, Ms Dunstan. You have been the reason for one of the million arguments my husband and I had over bringing up our baby. You know when they say that a baby can help make the relationship between spouses stronger? I think that applies only to happy or sleeping babies. A baby is so much work that it takes a toll on parents' physical and mental well-being. Sleep deprivation can render you irritable and make a total jerk out of you.

When our previous generations had babies, men did not do much of the baby work like changing diapers and mostly women were responsible for pacifying a crying baby.

In our times most dads are equal parents when it comes to sharing baby responsibilities, which is good. But now, since both husband and wife are equally involved, they have an opinion on everything. And more often than not, there is a difference in the two opinions.

I ranged in extreme feelings for my husband. I don't think I have loved him more than I did when we became parents. But I don't think I have hated him more than I did when we became parents. In a moment I'd thank heavens to have a husband who walked our baby for hours at 3 in the morning just so I could sleep peacefully at night. The very next day I'd yell at him for wanting to put his feet up after a long day at work when the baby had been driving me nuts the whole day.

With a baby the household chores multiply like bacteria. Even if you have domestic help, there is stuff to do ALL THE TIME. It is as if a giant electronic mixer full up to its brim is running continuously in your house without a lid on top. Baby things copulate and give rise to more baby things, resulting in more clutter and more cleaning every day. Division of those chores used to be a major reason for our fights, and it still is. And god forbid if that baby falls sick, the whole house is turned upside down. Those days feel so much longer, as if time has stopped. When my son got diarrhoea for the first time, after a week of scarlet fever, it lasted for one full month. One full month of forcing the rehydrating liquid into him that he would just not take, one full month of a dozen diapers a day and one full month of holding him while he slept at night. His colds lasted for weeks and his teething made him crazy annoyed. His first vaccinations made him whimper the whole night. Then there were those horrifying poxes that meant he would not eat or drink anything for days without crying.

Take those babies to a place where there are more than one of them and they will wake up in the middle of the night with a fever or tummy bug. They are the favourite feasts for any virus or any mosquito doing rounds and antibiotics are their best friends forever. If there is anything more difficult than parenting, it is parenting a sick baby. Nothing builds your fortitude more than that. It breaks your heart to see your child suffer and not be able to tell you what is bothering him.

Now the husband is one extremely workaholic animal. So he works late nights, works on weekends, travels for work and generally got to spend way less time than I did with our baby. My mother and mother-in-law were there with me, sequentially for the first two months of my son's life. After that I was all on my own, tending to the baby and trying to keep both of us alive through the day in my pajamas from the previous night.

Everyone tells you to 'sleep when the baby sleeps'. So should you also shower when the baby showers, defecate when the baby defecates and cook when the baby cooks? Really, is there nothing else for the mom to do in the day apart from baby things? I am not talking about amusement activities here, but even the daily basics of an adult outnumber those of the baby who is nothing but an eat-poop-sleep machine during his first few months.

During the fussy growth spurts and other general

discomforting times, there were days in a row when I longed to step out of the house or lock myself under a hot shower, like forever. The blissful moments were few and far in between, while the urge to pull out my hair was much more during those days. Add to that the previous evening's bickering with the husband and I found it hard to get through the day without blowing my top. Sometimes the squabbles only required an exchange of two sentences, albeit below the belt, to spray the whole house in a mist of tension. Something like:

'You can sleep peacefully at home; at least you don't have to go to work,' was his below the belt remark.

'And what do you do at work, check Facebook?' was my typical unsportsmanlike retort.

Few days after an incident like above, I would still be reeling from it and continuing with my silent treatment to him, who would then ask, 'At least tell me why you are mad at me?'

'You really don't know? And you expect me to not be mad at you?'

'Can you stop this psychological warfare with me?'

'How about I stop any sort of verbal communication with you?'

'Umm, I think you may have already done that.'

'Okay, then that's how it would be from now on. Let's just exchange emails about baby stuff. That is the only thing common between the two of us right now anyway.'

Even our casual banter on a Saturday afternoon sounded like this:

'So, in the last two months, it has been clearly established that we don't really need you to get us through the day.'

'That is brilliant! So I can play my match today then?'

'I am only saying how unimportant you are now. And no, you can't play that match.'

'Come on now. You can't ignore my contributions in the whole scheme of things.'

'Name one,' I asked.

'Like bringing our son into this world?'

'You did?'

'So, you did?'

'Yes, of course you did. When the stork came knocking at our door to deliver the baby, you called out for me from the couch to open the door, right? That is how big your contribution was in the "whole scheme of things" as you say,' I replied making air quotes with my fingers and added, 'as they say, "they also serve who sit—on the couch—and wait."'

'Well, well. I have more than compensated for my biological incompetence to birth him with my above and beyond readiness to serve him.'

'"Serve him?" Is he a tiny dictator? You know what? You are right, he is one. That should go on his T-shirt.'

'Well you can see the results of my "servitude" for yourself. He likes me more than you.' And, with that he pressed my most sensitive button.

It was true. My baby would treat me like a pariah the moment his dad appeared in the evening, and at two years, he does that even more. This is officially the final nail in my 'life's not fair' coffin.

I am not complaining when I say that I have had to work really hard, what with marathon feeding sessions and staying up late at night with the baby when Hubby had that really important meeting the next morning. Or maybe, I am complaining a tad. But I still wouldn't trade motherhood for anything. However, I would for once, really like to live the life of a dad. Just for the reason that despite all that jarring work we moms put in the whole day long, it is the dads who come across as the 'cooler' parent at the end of the day.

While I sterilized my baby's plastic rattle thrice, Hubby was handing him the obviously more interesting and full-of-germs car keys to play with. While I sanitized my hands so much that my skin peeled off, Hubby would just pick him up in a natural gush of love with curry stained hands to give him airplane rides and was rewarded with a cackling laughter. While I scraped the internet to inculcate good sleeping habit in my son, Hubby would just make him sleep on his tummy for hours. While I stressed out if our son was meeting his milestones, Hubby took pride in the fact that he was raising an absolutely awesome kid.

Moms parent with their brains and dads parent with their guts. Moms follow the instructions on the back of a board game and dads create a new game out of hurling the dice on the wall. I was there with my son the whole day jumping like a horse to entertain him. But the moment Hubby walked in, his eyes would light up. They still do. He may sound upset if I leave him, but he will squeal with joy if he sees his dad. The moment he hears someone unlocking the door of our house from outside in the evening, he drops everything and runs to see his father. If he is sleeping with me, with Hubby sleeping in another room, he will wake up in the middle of the night and walk over to his dad's bed. He never does that when I sleep in a different room! He will not throw even half of the tantrums with his dad that he throws with me. To which I often get, 'Because you let him do what he wants. He knows he can have his way with you, so he takes you for granted,' from the hubby. Surprise! Once again, it is my fault.

Soon this will turn into both the boys teaming up to watch a football match while I set the table for dinner or do some other mundane, unappreciated activity that no one wants to be a part of. I can already foresee that while I am away, Hubby will be raising our son on a diet of Coke and potato chips, letting him stay glued to the TV the whole day. Now obviously, he will come across as the better parent to my son.

Sigh. People should not call us the fairer sex when the world isn't fair to us. They should, in fact, compensate us all by doing the following:

- ☆ Build wax statues in our honour. (And make sure our baby fat doesn't show in them.)
- ☆ Permanently wire the brains of our children and husbands with the decisive answer of 'Because Mommy said so' to everything they question in the house.
- ☆ Ban all sports channels permanently.
- ☆ Make it punishable by law when any child or his

dad does not answer the frantic call of 'Come here and do this'.

☆ 'Who do you love the most? Mama or Papa?' should unequivocally and always be replied with: 'Mama', followed by, 'obviously'.

☆ Every day for two hours the family should act as if Mommy lives in a galaxy far, far away and hence can't be bothered with locating missing lone socks or other such earth shattering issues. (Wax statues may be used for motivation during those trying times.)

☆ Time spent sleeping by Mommy should be excluded from the above two hours.

☆ Publishing calorie content on ice cream tubs should be deemed illegal.

That should just about do it for now.

Dearly Beloved Sleep,
I Hope We Shall Meet Again Someday

Weeks became months and nights literally became days, when we hit the four-month mark. My son was still far away from sleeping well at night. If motherhood is an experiment to prove that sleep is not vital for a human to survive, I have been producing pretty favourable results.

Now babies, as you all might know, don't sleep (when you want them to, that is). That's it. They just don't. I can tell you more about that and you can read a gazillion books on baby sleep, but that really is the gist of it all. During the nine months that babies spend inside their mothers' tummies, they keep practising all the biological functions. So by the time they come out, they are expert sucklers, poopers, burpers and farters. (No, it wasn't your husband who just farted so loudly, it was your own cherub. It is possible for them to do that at that age and with that face.)

The one thing that those babies don't learn, and leave for

their parents to figure out, is sleeping on their own. I think they do that on purpose—because if they don't sleep, their parents don't sleep. And lack of sleep is one of the nastiest things for those poor parents to live with—day in and day out. Of course bringing babies up was never a day only job, the parents know that when they sign up for it. But babies want to rub that fact strongly in.

For babies, unlike for their parents, sleep is a highly overrated activity when there is so much else to do in the world—chewing on the TV remote or looking at the bread crusts fallen on the floor, for example. This new world is like an Eastman colour musical movie to them compared to the black-and-white womb they were in. They are just about done jumping from their bouncers to see how a door opens and shuts, when we up the game with our tablets and phones—taking stimulation to the next level altogether.

Not only did my son almost hate sleep, he also didn't know what to do when he was sleepy. He was for sure uncomfortable when he was tired, but he didn't know if falling asleep was what he should be doing. For an adult, the process is very simple—feel sleepy, yawn, hit the bed, snore. For my son it went like—feel sleepy, rub eyes, yawn, hear the door bell, get excited, ask to be taken to the door, observe and form another connection in his tiny brain, forget about sleeping, start playing, feel sleepy again, rub eyes, get tired, know not what to do now, cry, resist everything.

The process would loop for some time with different observations in each run, filling his head with new ideas each time. Finally, when at his tether's end of weariness, he would settle in our arms and ask in his own way to help him go to sleep. He was such a motion junkie that he needed the earth under him to literally move and spin his head into drowsiness. We would rock or swing him for hours. I can safely say that Rome was definitely built faster than the time it used to take for my son to summon the sandman every night. And the minute we'd put him down in the bed, completely asleep, he would wake up, as if he was saying, 'Get back to work here mister, we are not done yet!'

Once when we took him outdoors, he fell asleep in his stroller and we thought we'd cracked the code. From then on every time he felt sleepy, we'd put him in the stroller and depending on the time of the day, we either took him out or kept pushing the stroller in our living room while watching TV on mute. The moment he made some sound, we'd push the stroller again. I used to have dreams about an eighteen-year-old him insisting on sleeping in a stroller and me not being able to find one big enough to fit him in. But for now, I was happy whichever way he slept. He still took an hour to fall asleep, but at least we could save our backs by just wheeling him around the house with one hand and still have the other hand free to WhatsApp our friends with.

So, with his day naps sorted, we still had the mammoth task of tackling the bad boy of multiple night wake ups. Hubby and I wished each other good luck instead of good night every night when we went in the room to put him to sleep. We went all armed with water, snacks, earphones, phone, laptop, iPad, chargers, overdue utility bills, nail polish, pedicure kit, face pack, hardbound copies of *Anna*

Karenina and similar never ending books, warm socks and other camping equipment to keep us company during our ordeal. We never knew for how long we'd be in there. His bedtime was way earlier than ours, so we couldn't sleep with him. A lot of times, for hours we couldn't dare to pull our arm from under his head as he slept, lest he should wake up. We took turns to sleep with him, so at least one of us could sleep peacefully for a few hours and then pass the baton to the other when baby woke up—like 166 times in a night.

Whoever coined the phrase 'sleeping like a baby' never had a baby of his own. My son, a true blue baby complete with tummy rolls and that naturally delicious baby smell that should be preserved, has never slept like a 'baby', so to speak. He used to wake up by the slightest sound of a drawer shingle. So, we didn't use the bathroom next to his room, and if need be, flushed the toilet very gently, lest it should disturb his sleep. I am certain that even the shutting of my eyelids woke him up as I dared to put my head down while he was asleep.

So I thought that this is how babies generally are and that eventually they grow out of it. He was only waking up crying every few hours during the night and I only had to sit upright holding him from 4 in the morning when he would ditch the stroller. Only once had I put a juice carton in the washing machine and thrown house keys in the trash bin—so I was still coping up well with the sleep deprivation. Perhaps my son was just going through a phase, I told myself, like that very popular four month-sleep regression that I had read about—when babies suddenly stopped sleeping well at four months—if at all they had ever started to sleep well before. So it could only get better from here, I thought.

Turned out that my son was in a perpetual sleep regression phase. Even over a month later he was still at his wakeful and sleep fighting best. The day to join work was getting near so I feared it would be difficult for me to carry on like this. My office didn't have a washing machine where I could safely place my juice carton. I started to feel that I was doing something terribly wrong which had now resulted in my son's horrible sleeping habits. Why doesn't he sleep like all other babies his age?

I talked to my paediatrician and she suggested that I feed my son a bottle of formula over and top of his last nursing session at night and then if he still woke up, give him water. The idea was that he will learn that waking up isn't all that cool after all, if all you get is plain water in a plastic bottle. So one night, I gave him a lavender bath, which I had read induced sleep. (You see, by now I would have even trusted that frog in my neighbourhood pond if he'd croaked up to me about a way to make my son sleep.)

An hour after nursing him, I gave him a formula bottle. He resisted on finishing it, but after a few nudges he did man up and downed the whole thing. Only to wake up in the night with the worst tummy ache of his entire life, that continued until the next day. 'Not happening again,' I told myself, after verbally kicking that doctor and physically kicking my own behind.

At the same time, I came across stories of moms on online baby forums who said that their babies were sleeping through the night at the same age—some even right from day three. They were all gallantly sharing tales on how well they had trained their babies to sleep by setting a bedtime routine and how well their children behaved exactly like the ones in the advertisements for sleep-inducing toys. I had joined these forums during my pregnancy and I felt secure to find so many women like me expecting babies at around the same time as I was. It was like being in a kitty party on an island away from the world. An island comprising only big bellies and swollen feet. Sharing jokes about sagging bodies that no one else would ever laugh at. Posting pictures. Writing birth stories. Spreading memes like, 'I am so tired that…I got jealous of my computer when it went to sleep' and 'I am so tired that…I got tired again today—I am re-tired'.

There were moms on these forums who had been there and done that, and there were moms who were taking baby steps with their first babies. They welcomed questions about your baby's diaper content in all graphic details. They assured you that you were not alone, even though the village that had once existed to bring a child up was not there anymore. A generation of high rises and low support, we were all raising our children one-to-one behind closed doors and with the virtual support of internet strangers. Even if we did have our moms and moms-in-law around, we were too cool to listen to them, since they had babies in the days of yore—the pre-Google era.

Apart from giving an overload of information, those forums also served as a great source of entertainment, what with exotic four-worded username mommies pawning their brains in public. Once, at one of the forums, an *inspired_by_barbie_123* had asked, 'If I change the ringtone of my phone, will my baby not like it?' To which *mamaofsixandcounting* had replied suggesting that *inspired_by_barbie_123* should perhaps try different ringtones first and check for her baby's reaction before deciding which one to go with. There was also one *luv_ma_hubby_till_tomorrow* who had once asked if it was okay to do the 'dance' with her hubby three months postpartum, where dance was code for love-making.

I am not making up these agonies and confessions.

In fact, I am quite embarrassed to tell you what all I have asked on the forums at least once. Here goes my list: (The italicized text below is what I interpret of it all now, since I am much wiser and writing books that won't teach you parenting. The list below is not exhaustive. But I had overrun my quota for self-deprecation by the end of it.)

☆ My baby is diagnosed with scarlet fever. Doctor <*who is highly qualified and spent years in a med school*> has prescribed antibiotics. What is your opinion on that, <*dear fellow, never been to medical school, a complete stranger, might as well be serial killer in real life for all you know*> mommies?

☆ I think my baby feels cold at night. How should I dress him up? <*Will it be okay to use some...er... common sense there?*>

☆ I think I overdressed my baby last night. Does that make me a bad mother? <*Because that really is the worst thing for anyone to have ever done to their baby, except perhaps letting them eat dog food. Does hell have a place for me?>*

☆ Seriously, how do you dress them up when you take them out in the cold? *<They still don't make babies with LED indicators to tell us if they are hot or cold? Is this the eighteenth century or what?>*

☆ Have you ever washed stuffed animal toys in the washing machine and dried them in a dryer, and they came out fine? *<Because I was thinking they might get extinct from this planet if I did that. Or at the very least, I fear that my son's favourite 'Flutter the Butterfly' might just undergo a reverse evolution and turn into a caterpillar.>*

☆ The twelve-week growth spurt in babies is when the twelfth week starts (completion of eleven weeks), or when the twelfth week finishes and the thirteenth starts? *<Since I need to take out my baby behaviour combating gear according to his exact age, down to how many minutes and seconds he is old on that day. Also, will my baby be a nerd too?>*

☆ So I started my baby on carrots today. How much should I give him? Do I measure in number of carrots or spoons? What sized spoons? *<Will the size of my brain do, or I need one even smaller?>*

☆ While lying in my lap on his back, my son joins his hands together and lifts his upper body up, sometimes together with legs, almost trying to fold himself up. He does this several times. Has anyone else seen this? What does this mean? *<That he is*

> *trying to communicate something metaphysical and surreal through his body language or that I have given birth to an alien?>*

☆ My three-month-old is spitting more than usual, otherwise acting normal. *<Should I call the ambulance, maybe?>*

☆ Did anyone's LO learn to sleep on their own? DS only sleeps when DH rocks him. He is EBF, except very rarely FF. *<Did you see me flaunt my forum lingo here?*>*

So naturally, to tackle the biggest issue of my life about my son's non-sleeping, I had again turned to these forums for help. The achiever mommies here suggested me to try different sleeping positions, sleep routines, sleeping areas, extra snugly sleeping bags, sleep toys and whatever else that had worked for them. I did them all. If sleeping babies was an industry, I was their prime target segment.

But nothing worked for us.

Someone once suggested me to replicate my son's enclosed stroller environment on his bed by making a castle of pillows around him. It meant that I had to guard those pillows like a hawk from falling over his face the whole night and hence it defeated the whole purpose of me getting

---

*This is what those abbreviations stand for that you use in forums— LO: Little One, DS: Darling Son, DH: Darling Husband, EBF: Exclusively Breast Fed, FF: Formula Fed, etc. Takes a little practice and you are a pro. A few months down the road, and I was rattling those out in my sleep to other mommies on forums.

peaceful sleep. Another time I was advised to put my spit, milk, sweat stained shirt that was two-day old in his bed next to his nose to trick him into thinking I was still with him. To enhance the effect further, I had recorded that buzzing sound in my phone—the one I used to make when making him fall asleep—and put it next to his ear to play the whole night. That seemed to be working for some time until it automatically moved to the next track of Shakira's *Waka Waka* on the phone's playlist and scared the living daylights out of him.

When all above failed, I was told that white noise worked as a charm for making babies sleep. You know, like the noise of a tumble dryer or washing machine and in my son's case, a hairdryer. There is no melody in that but that sound is very similar to what babies are used to hearing inside the womb, so it soothes them. And it helps to mask all other sounds—the doorbell for example. I relied on my hairdryer running full blast for weeks, before it finally broke down.

Then I bought another one.

Since babies have very definite sleep cycles, (in my son's case, it was exactly 45 minutes before he woke up again), the hairdryer had to be kept on all the while to help him jump through the cycles. But soon he outgrew of that too.

By now I was only short of shooting my son with a tranquilizer gun to make him sleep—that poor little baby.

The one thing that I didn't want to try, even when many parents swore by it, was the very popular *Cry it Out* method—leaving babies to cry themselves to sleep and checking on them every now and then, until they learnt how to sleep on their own. It was too harsh for my chickenheart to handle. Secretly, I was also sure that it wouldn't work on my baby and the guilt of making my baby cry would make me gouge out my own eyes with his baby spoon the very next morning. (I had sterilized the spoon twice after washing though, just in case.)

I did try the other, *Put Up, Put Down* method of sleep training that I had read about, when my husband was away on a business trip. This one required making the babies sleep in your arms like normal until they were drowsy and almost asleep but still awake, and then putting them down in the bed so they learned to do the final act of sleeping on their own. If the baby cried when you put him down, you were supposed to pick him back up and do the whole routine for as many times as it took. By doing this, they eventually learned to sleep on their own and stopped waking up at night.

'So this sounds doable,' I thought. 'I mean I am not leaving him to cry on his own in the dark and I am still teaching him a skill. A skill to sleep on his own! He will be grateful to me one day for having taught him that!'

So we started.

7.30 p.m.
Sleepy time check
Bedtime routine shebang check
Lullaby check
Rocking check
Baby drowsy check

Put him down check
Baby cries check
Pick him up check
Baby calms down check
Put him down check
Baby cries check
Pick him up check
Once
Twice
Tenth time
Won't give up
Roll up sleeves check
Wipe sweat from forehead check
9.30 p.m.
Thirty-second time
Pick him up check
Baby calms down check
Put him down check
Still going strong
1.00 a.m.
Eighty bloody sixth time
Pick him up check
Baby calms down check
Put him down check
Baby cries check
Pick him up check
Mommy's back broken
Baby, Mommy both passed out on the bed.
Check, check, check.

And that was the end of our sleep training saga.

Interestingly, after all that rigmarole, the odd nights that my son did sleep for seven straight hours (there were exactly three of those nights, as I remember doing the happy dance the next morning), I could not sleep well, as my body was now so used to waking up. And I found that I actually missed him when he slept longer than usual hours. He was still at his hyper active best even after the rough nights, and he was growing just fine.

In fact, he was growing way too quickly and it suddenly struck me that soon he will not need me to comfort and kiss him when he woke up at night.

I realized that the reason I stressed about my son's sleeping habits was more to do with the fact that he wasn't doing what he was supposed to do, than it was for me getting a good night's sleep.

It is a tough world these days to be a baby, especially in the case of first-time parents. There is so much information available to help you do parenting 'right'—completely measured and verified by experts. There are people evaluating your performance. And behind all of that is a mommy who is pretty darn sure she has been doing everything wrong.

In older times babies had quite a chilled out life. They were fed when they wanted, they were made to sleep when they wanted and they played with whatever was around even if it did not enhance their gross motor or sensory skills. That pretty much summed up their day. They didn't have to wiggle their tiny necks through designer collared shirts while going out and they absolutely were never made to wear tuxedos. (Seriously, the stuff we make them do for Facebook photos these days!) There were no averages to benchmark their growth against. They got dirty, they fell, and they thrived—in a world where there were bigger dangers than BPA-laden plastic cups.

Cut to the modern times, and it feels like babies are part of a mediocre sci-fi movie set in the future. Their meals are packaged in tiny jars, their diapers have indicators to tell if it is time to change, their toys flash lights and play music like gizmos, their bodies are strapped in bouncy seats, their houses are baby-proofed, their movements are captured by video monitors and their routines are programmed—as advised by the parenting experts. Now all they have to say is, 'Beam us up, Scotty!'

While reading all that parenting literature, I never realized how much pressure it was adding to my brain. A lot of that information that I gathered, projected babies as a collective race. You know, like the amphibians or the Xulu tribe. So, by this age babies should be having this amount of milk. By that age babies should be sleeping through the night. By this age babies should be able to spell hippopotamus and stand on one leg. That, if they do not accomplish these, they are way behind their milestones of complex linguistics and acrobatic skills, and you, a parenting failure. There is this unnecessary urge to make your baby function like ideal—where ideal is defined by some book, an internet article or through the voices of mommies on online forums. I now realize that in our effort to raise a child who sleeps well, eats all greens, plays with all toys that we buy; we sometimes forget that he is a human too. A human just like us, who has his preferences and temperament.

When was the last time we ate or slept according to a book? Is there even a book like that for adults? Why do we then hold those little ones to such high standards of performance? Sure, they need to be taught what is good for them, but only when they are a little bigger to reason or talk even. Some experts suggest that by six months babies have no need to wake up in the night. That, babies are little manipulators who know how to get their way if we give in. That, if we do what they want us to do when they wake up, we will be 'rewarding' their wake ups and they will never learn to stay asleep. And what 'rewards' are those materialistic babies seeking—a cuddle? A milk bottle? A chance to snuggle into parents' bed? The reassuring voice of their mothers? Is that really too much to give them? Will they ask for it when they are eighteen? Won't we miss it then?

So, one fine day, wisdom dawned on me and I decided to stop reading about baby sleep related stuff on the internet. At the forum that I was a part of, someone mentioned that they had fed sliced carrots to their baby which came out intact in his poop. That indeed was my lowest point on the forum. There was a certain limit that my virtual voyeurism and love for baby biology could stoop down to. So I quit the forum too, ran for my life and never looked back. Life has become much happier ever since.

Now my son still doesn't sleep through the night even at the age of two, and needs a cuddle a few times to drift back to wonderland, but I am okay with it. I don't have much choice there anyway. Besides, if you sleep, you miss on watching them giggle through their sleep at some funny dream or such—and that is quite a sight to enjoy even at the most unearthly hour.

(Or so I console myself with the sour grapes my baby gives me from his plate—completely organic, seedless, BPA-free, each one individually picked by a brand new grape-clutching machine, peeled and sliced to the exact size as recommended for babies in the *Exemplary Journal of Parenting for Raising Perfect Babies*. What? You haven't read that one? And you are still not feeding your baby grapes and denying him of all the awesome flavonoids and antioxidants that come with them? Go on and do it right now, before that woman who has never had a baby of her own judges you on your parenting skills!)

The Day(s)care Saga or How Babies Trap You Out of Your Own Will

Ever since I finished studies, I have been working. The single most driving factor of my life has been work. The one that decided which country I lived in, where I spent a large part of my day or what I looked forward to. With every year, every appraisal, every job change, I have been adding lines to my CV (and to my forehead), working and reworking all of that to fit into two pages. If anyone asked me to introduce myself, I'd tell them what my name was and what I did for a living, sometimes appending the sentence with the degrees I had earned that had led me to the jobs I did.

Even on a few months in-between job break that I once had, many years before I got pregnant, I hardly did anything worthwhile with my time, except for figuring out which job I would take next. By about 4 p.m. in the day, on that break, I would go completely berserk having done nothing. So I would turn to YouTube to listen to ghazals about Heer getting married to some rich bloke and leaving Ranjha crying for life. And I felt depressed about that mythical Ranjha dude and wondered if I could help him somehow. Now I did have a lot of hobbies to keep me occupied, but hobbies didn't accomplish anything. They didn't make sales figures for the quarter or helped me get my annual bonus. If I went swimming, I just did some leisurely laps and not like I was training to cross the English Channel. If I read a book, I didn't have to critique it for a paid review. The activities were just to fill the day and not aim for any future goal. The days at home meant I didn't have to shower, iron my clothes or put on make-up. Because, what was the point of doing that if my only outing during the day would be to buy a can opener for those tomato puree tins I had bought the day before on a similar outing?

If you have worked for over a decade, suddenly sitting at home during a weekday without any holiday or sickness can feel rather odd. While the rest of the world is continuing its regular course of action—earth moving around the sun, governments falling, property prices soaring, people running to catch buses to go to work—you feel as if you have stopped short abruptly and are being left out of the race. I mean, what is a day without coffee corner gossip with colleagues and existential-anxiety doubts playing in your head when you fill some dumb spreadsheet at work!? The whole environment around your house on a weekday is so painfully dull. The incomprehensible chatter of school children in the afternoons gets to you. Emphatic blonde women with fake abs, selling you even faker tummy tuck machines in infomercials, is just about all the passion you see during the day.

It was hard for me to imagine my whole life like that. My brain was so wired to get up in the morning, get late for work, waste time on the internet, rush to meet deadlines at work, count days until Friday and feel suicidal on a Monday morning—that I couldn't imagine sitting at home. So, quitting my job to raise my kid was never an option. What would I do once he goes to school and then to his painting and taekwondo classes? What would I fill up my day with? I could take a break for a few years and then resume work. But by then the world would have moved on, and finding a job again would be that much more difficult and frustrating.

I had worked hard through my pregnancy to achieve my annual targets in the six months I had that year before I went to have my baby. I wanted that promotion so bad. I was interviewing with other companies if they had a better job, even offering them to move across continents for the job if the job was too good to refuse. Perhaps, all this while, I was conveniently forgetting that the baby parked inside me would exit one day and lug onto me—literally or metaphorically—for almost the rest of my working life.

My boss said to me that once I have a baby I wouldn't be this career-oriented. And I sniggered at her. Another vice president at my organization and a mother of three advised that it might be good for me to get back to my current job, which I could do with my eyes closed. Being able to just do the job optimally sans any starry performance was going to be hard enough after a baby, she told me. So I should not think of taking up any new challenges. Of course that old woman didn't know what I was capable of, I had told myself.

Just before I left for my maternity leave; after flowers, sham hugs and a lunch thrown by my boss, I put my name label on my office chair, lest anyone should usurp it while I was gone. I thought of my maternity leave like a slightly longer than usual annual holiday, where I would spring back to normal after a few months and get cracking on that promotion or that next awesome assignment like a superwoman with a crisply-ironed cape.

I couldn't have been more wrong—about being able to iron my cape (and other clothes for that matter), or about myself in general.

Not only did I not have any energy left in me to do all of that, but also, strangely, I did not have the will. If I come to think of it, motherhood almost turned me from a job-hopping and working-for-bonus capitalist into a let's-exchange-our-babies'-pictures and let's-go-home-early-to-be-with-family socialist. Soon I was this agony aunt my female colleagues had started turning to for discussing their boyfriend or infertility problems. And I loved that! I wanted to help anyone and everyone around me, with a special place in my heart for fellow parents or parents-to-be. People had also stopped using swear words when I was around, since I was now considered to be too motherly to appreciate any kind of profanity.

I had started participating in all women events at work,

which earlier I used to find too, well, womanish for my taste. These were events like Mother's Day celebrations or seminars on gender equality and how to make the workplace better for mothers. Before pregnancy, I would attend those only if they offered me a chance to network with senior officials for better career prospects. But now, I was signing petitions for woman rights and brainstorming on how to make lactation rooms more comfortable for mothers at work. I was proposing radical ideas like being able to bring children to work or having half work days, although they were immediately shot down by my non-maternal seniors. My PowerPoint presentations to a new audience had a picture of my baby and me on the first slide as a way to introduce myself. It just felt too selfish to include my solo picture there, or anywhere else on social media for that matter. The baby might just feel left out if I did that. He was a part of my identity and I wanted to make that point clear to the whole world.

My work—life balance had heavily tilted towards life now. If I found myself stressing out at work, all I had to do was to realize that in a few hours I'd be home cuddling with my baby, or to go to the bathroom to watch his videos.

Once, when there were hardly any people in the office, I took my phone with me to the loo and turned Baby's video on without muting it.

'*Ta ta ta ta ta ta ta,*' baby captured in my phone was babbling away to glory.

'You are such a cute baby. Yes you are. Yes you are,' I talked back to the screen.

'*Bub bub bub bub bub,*' Baby continued.

'Yes, Mama loves you my poochie pie. Yes she does. Yes she does.'

'*Babababadoobeeeee.*'

'*Babababadoobeeeee* to you too baby! See you soon!'

As soon as the video got over I heard chuckles from some ladies outside. Whoopsy daisy! They had been listening to my private motherese all this while! Too embarrassed to face them, I continued to stay behind shut doors for 20 minutes, opened the door slightly to see if it was all clear outside and walked out as nonchalantly as possible.

Interestingly enough, I couldn't associate with other colleagues when they seemed extremely overworked or anxious at work for some reason. I just wanted to tell all of them to have babies and be happy in life—it was okay to not accomplish your targets some times. But of course, you can never voice your feelings out loud at work, which is another reason to spend more time at home.

Colleague sitting next to me (talking to herself): 'Damn, I am royally screwed!'

Me (ignoring the colleague's mumbling): 'Hey, the photographer just emailed me my son's new pictures. They are great. Want to have a look?'

Colleague (politely obliging and looking at my computer for a split second before turning away): 'Um, yes. Wow, those are really great. But sorry, I have to attend to something urgently.'

Me: 'Oh sure, please go ahead.'

Colleague (muttering to herself and stomping her feet):

'Shit Shit Shit. I wasn't supposed to send that email out so soon. What do I do now? Sorry, excuse my language.'

Me (smiling for the next 30 minutes): 'He does look really cute. Hey, I need to go pee-pee before we go for lunch, okay?'

Colleague (baffled at my use of words and in a typical hoity-toity manner): 'Sorry?'

Me: 'Oh, I meant I need to visit the washroom first before we go for lunch, okay?'

Colleague: 'Sure. I didn't realize it was already lunch time.'

Before having a baby, I was that colleague, and now I was that weird lady next to her who showed everyone her baby's photographs. My life had taken a complete U-turn.

My first few days back at work went all fine and dandy. Husband and I alternately worked half days from home while still looking after the baby. But we couldn't continue with this arrangement forever. My parents or in-laws coming from India and staying with us to tend to the baby for long-term was not feasible. I did not want to hire any nanny or housemaid to take care of my son, as I had massive trust issues there. If I did that, I would have had to install a spy camera in every corner of my house that I'd watch like a hawk every minute from work. I could totally picture myself yelling right at the camera from my office kilometres away, 'Don't pick the baby with that angle of your arms!' or 'Why did you to go the bathroom?'

Hence the only permanent option we were left with was to send our son to a daycare. Of course the trust issue was still there. (But that paranoid, control-freak self at times even worked with the husband when I left the baby in his care, suspecting him of not doing everything the 'mom' way.) At least, with the daycare, the accountability was better, since there were a lot of children and a lot of caretakers available. You could walk in any time unannounced and make alliances with fellow parents to gang up against the daycare if things didn't go well.

So we enrolled our son into one of the highly recommended daycares in town. The weekend before he had to start there, I worked on writing his user manual for the daycare people to follow.

I did tell you earlier that I was a nerd, right?

So the user manual—which I almost expected those guys to print out, laminate and stick on the walls—had clear directions around all the activities that consumed my baby the whole day.

This is close to what it looked like:

Feeding:

☆ *Every 3–3.5 hours—90–120 ml formula. I can't give you an exact amount; you will need to see what works. Don't overfeed him and don't starve him and you should be good to go. (I know you are tempted to say 'duh' here, but I stopped caring about such things since I became a mother.)*
☆ *Baby may cry sometimes even after bottle is finished and you take the bottle away. This can mean two things: One, he just wants to suck on the empty bottle for some time. Two, if he continues to cry, he needs more formula. So you*

should keep a backup bottle ready. Preferably, a backup of the backup too, as he is a bit impatient in matters related to his stomach—both ingoing and outgoing.

...

Sleeping:

☆ *Baby takes at least two naps in the day and wakes up exactly after 45 minutes to be put back to sleep again. I suggest keeping one caretaker dedicated to that task and set alarms for 45 minutes so you are ready to act on time.*
☆ *He cries when very sleepy.*
☆ *He makes faint cries when he is almost about to sleep.*
☆ *There is a subtle difference between the above two, so it needs to be assessed carefully. (Refer to the next section for more details on crying.)*

...

Decoding Crying:

☆ *Repetitive screams like that of a hairy woman getting her first wax, means that he needs to be burped.*
☆ *Off and on indecisive cries when he is playing, means that he is bored with the current activity. If crying continues even after changing the activity, he is tired and wants to sleep. Refer to the previous section on sleep for more guidelines in that area.*
☆ *Loud, continuous crying like a fire brigade siren along with tears, means that he is either very hungry or in some kind*

of pain. I would appreciate if we don't reach that stage.

☆ *You can try to soothe baby by picking him close in your arms and walking outdoors and showing him some animal. If you can't find one, then get down on all fours and pretend to be one. Preferably a cat. Stripey is better.*

☆ *If you are unable to soothe him, the maximum time you should wait before calling me = 1 minute. If my phone is engaged, as I will invariably be calling you at that time, call my husband right away.*

• • •

It went on like this for about fourteen pages, until I was completely sure I had included the last bit of detail in there. I had to be content that I was handing the project over to someone else with all the documentation required to run it seamlessly.

The daycare was close to my office and because of the latest flexi-work policy, it was relatively easier than before for me to sneak out and work from anywhere. I could, for example, drop in at lunch time to see him and nurse him. So everything was sorted. Now, all that my son had to do was to get dropped off in the morning, take a morning nap, eat, play with other children, smile, learn new skills and have fun. Soon it would be time for me to pick him up after a highly productive work day, where he would greet me with a big grin and get a big hug in return. And I would sleep peacefully in the night with the assurance that I have got my life all together. Perfect as a dream.

Except it didn't happen like that.

Day 0: The interview day: Hubby, baby and I reached the daycare. The caregivers asked us to finish some admin formalities and a form about baby's details, similar to the ones in my bespoke baby user manual, but shrunk in detail by almost fifty times. I am sure my son sensed something right then. This was the first ever place he had gone to in his senses that was full of so much commotion. There were a lot of giant people walking in with little people, but walking out alone after some time. Where did the little people disappear after all? His eyes were wide open, looking around in every direction like a meerkat hanging in his daddy's arms. A little while later, they took us to the actual room where he was supposed to spend his day. The room was full of toys, cupboards, noisy children and a special corner for him with a swing and bouncy seat, as he was the only baby in the group who could not even crawl yet and needed to lie down the entire day. His corner was demarcated with a very low plastic fence, so bigger children could not enter there, but he could still see all the action from his abode. The bedroom was right next to this playroom that had little beds stacked on top of each other like bird cages.

That is where it hit me for the first time that my son was suddenly going to inhabit a new home altogether. Although I had seen the place a few times before, I had never pictured my son in that, playing on that floor and sleeping in that bed. My little birdie was actually going to step out of my nest. The tear gates opened. And how! I don't know what came on to me at that moment. It normally takes a bit of a build up for me to actually cry, but this was instant.

'I'm sorry,' said I to the caregiver, 'I don't know what is happening to me.'

'Oh, please don't be sorry. It is absolutely normal,' she replied feeling a bit apologetic.

Thankfully, my son was asleep then and we drove back home after finishing all formalities.

Day 1: The getting used to day: We had to stay for a couple of hours that day, minus Hubby. The moment we entered the room, we saw a few more children. Then a few more and a few more. All running from one place to the other. One with a runny nose too. A few were building a tower with blocks and some were hurling plastic cars at each other. All that noise wowed and scared my baby and he started crying. It was also the time for his morning nap so someone took him into the bedroom. The newness of the place made him even more awake and cranky. Soon he was given his milk bottle and he went calm. I took him home after that.

We thought we did great and high-fived.

Day 2: The getting independent day: So I was not allowed to stay at all now. I just had to hand him over to the caregiver, kiss and walk out. I did linger around the daycare premises, just in case. My son did not like anything that day. The stimulation was killing him and he was getting more tired and yet unable to fall asleep. They didn't rock him like we did at home, they didn't sing to him like we did at home, they didn't snuggle with him in bed like we did at home. They didn't come running to him when he snivelled. 'So that is what the outside world looks like,' my son must have thought—if he could think at that age and size. Originally scheduled to stay for four hours that day, I was called after two hours of caregivers trying to make him happy. We went home again.

Day 3: The real day: He had to stay there for the full day. He didn't have much sense of separation anxiety then, but he did see they didn't do things his way. He went on a hunger strike. No bottles for him! After about six hours of fasting since his last meal early morning, Hubby went running to him and gave him his bottle and took him home.

Day 4: The (surprise) stay-at-home day: Remember the runny nose child I told you about on the first day? He did my son in. My son woke up with cold and fever. No more daycare for my son that day. I called in sick too.

So that was our week one in the outside world. Things would be better the next week, we were told. So we braved again for full days this week. I could only call once in a day to check on him, but I had to let him stay there to let him get accustomed to the new place and people. He must have cried a lot there, I assumed. And here I was chewing my nails in office, trying to distract myself from him while waiting for the clock to move. I missed him terribly. It felt like a part of me was suddenly cut off and taken to a place far away. I missed rocking him to sleep, I missed making silly faces to him, I missed hearing the annoyingly repetitive sound of his musical mobile and watching his legs propel with that. I missed nom-noming on his roly-poly thighs. I missed having a captive audience in him to listen to my ranting about life, chapped lips, greying hair, reduced bonus and that annoying accounts guy at work. I even missed changing my baby's diapers—that is what motherhood does to you.

I was getting doubts in my mind if I was doing the right thing. I made frequent trips to the bathroom to just sit and ponder, and occasionally wet my eyes or look in the mirror to reassure myself. Meanwhile, my son's cold went from bad to worse. To add to the agony, his first tooth erupted in that week, and he had no idea how to deal with that pain (neither did I, for that matter). Hubby was away on a work trip and I just couldn't walk out of my meetings late in the day. By the last day of this week, he had completely lost his voice because of a stuffy chest and continuous coughing. I blamed myself for everything. Not that my son hadn't fallen ill before this, but I somehow thought that the house germs were better tamed and much more under my control. The daycare germs, on the other hand, were completely alien to me.

The next whole week he was sick and we both stayed at home. My boss was not very happy to have a highly distracted employee, who had barely spent four full days at work in the last two and a half weeks. She obviously cared a lot about making those quarter numbers. She wrote me an angry 'What the hell do you think you are doing?' kind of an email.

And here I was dealing with that classic mind vs heart debate. Logic told me that my son would eventually adjust in the daycare like every child does. In fact, the sooner he started, the better it would be. The daycare was excellent and so were the caretakers there. He would learn to be more independent and socialize with other kids. I was doing great in my career and a break would set me back in this tough market, or cost me my promotion at the very least.

But my heart kept saying that I wanted to stay at home with my son. Hubby told me that there was no point in going through all this if it didn't make me happy. You have to give him credit for reminding me of the most basic things in life, even when he himself forgets to put the toilet seat down.

So, one fine morning as I sat on the floor massaging my baby while my colleagues massaged their bosses' egos, I decided that this was what I wanted to do the whole day—just play mommy. It felt like I was living the purpose of my life by doing this. My career was turning into a distraction rather than a driving factor in my life.

I then blurted out rather rhetorically to the whole world—which included only of my baby and a TV playing in the background—holding the baby oil bottle up close to my mouth like a microphone.

'MY SON IS STILL TOO LITTLE TO BE GOING THROUGH ALL THIS. THE CAREGIVERS AT DAYCARE, NO MATTER HOW CARING THEY ARE, CANNOT TREAT HIM LIKE ANOTHER PAGE IN THEIR DAILY CHILDREN'S BOOKS THAT SAYS HOW MUCH HE ATE AND WHETHER HE HAD A POOPY DIAPER. I AND ONLY I OWN HIS POOPY DIAPERS. I WILL NOT, I REPEAT, I WILL NOT EXCHANGE A MINUTE OF HIS GROWING UP TO MAKE POWER POINTS AT WORK—ESPECIALLY NOT THE

ONES THAT MY BOSS MAKES ME DO TO PASS OFF AS HER OWN WORK.'

I then bowed to the audience and stepped down from the piano stool. After a moment of dumbstruck silence, President Obama stood up from the audience, wiped his tears and started to clap. Everyone else followed him, and the applause that followed was deafening.

Wait, that was on CNN.

Meanwhile in my real world, my son had rolled over his mattress to catch a dead bug on the floor.

Me: 'You ungrateful cheeky monkey! Can I get some appreciation here, at least a clap, or a smile, that tells me I am the best mom in the world?'

Baby: '*Bhurrrrrrrr.*'

Me: 'That's like my boy. Oh, it is nothing much son. You don't need to thank me. I am just doing my duty. Wait, did you just spit on me?'

Oh well. Nothing says 'I love you, Mom' like a blob of bonny clabber on your shoulder, freshly delivered by your baby.

So, just like that, I took the plunge and decided to continue being a stay-at-home mom.

(Little did I know that in that rush of emotion, I was signing myself up for the most difficult job of my whole goddamn life!)

Guess Which Job Is Tougher?
(Hint: It's the One Where You Don't Get Weekends Off)

stay·at·home·mom (SAHM)
/'sā,hēm/
Noun
1. A woman who lives in a perpetually messed up house and happily lets her child drive her nuts all day.
2. A woman who is not allowed to pee in peace.

Synonyms:
pro bono nanny, thankless domestic jobs doer, loony.

....

About eight months into the job and I came to realize that a SAHM is quite an interesting creature. She does what is possibly the most physically taxing and brain frying job in the whole family, and yet her efforts are the most undermined when compared to her other bread winning or bread wasting members of the family. A jaded Mother's Day card from Hallmark and a bunch of flowers just don't make up for her work. On the contrary, they just add to the clutter that she is never done cleaning up.

Flowers? Damn, I have to now find that godforsaken vase that is catching dust in one corner of the house. It is lying perhaps at the same place where all the critical toy pieces are hiding without which the toy is incomplete and hence rejected by the child right since the day you bought it. Then I have to clean that vase, fill it with water and place flowers in it. I will need to change water the next day and throw those flowers away when they are dead.

A card? One that has words written by a paid copywriter that you are passing on as your own feelings? I can't even throw that as it would be rude. So I have to find another place to keep it, or simply stack it on top of that pile of birthday cards I have received from my office colleagues over the past years, the ones that have about twenty signatures crowding a 4X4 size paper.

Thanks for adding to my work.

The rest 364 days, apart from Mother's Day, for a SAHM are as banal as they can get, where her contributions are conveniently forgotten in the whole scheme of things. On my first birthday after my baby was born; I started the day by wiping his butt and ended it with loading the dishwasher. I took him with me to a restaurant for lunch and had to leave even before I could smell the soup served to me. Clearly, it was time for him to wake up from his nap earlier than usual and throw his arms and legs everywhere in the stroller, since it was my birthday—not that the soup was more important than him in any way. There was a cake that I ordered myself and a present that I shopped online. Parents were far away and I hadn't found the time to call my friends in many light years. So they didn't bother turning up, much to my relief at not having to host them in my punch-drunk state. Even I wouldn't go to a birthday party where the host hadn't showered in two days and was yawning more frequently than she breathed. Facebook had forced a lot of my friends to wish me virtually, to which I did a 'To whomsoever it may concern, thanks a lot for wishing me' kind of PA announcement-reply to save time. Some even sent me e-greetings that took longer to open than I could sit comfortably for without the baby needing my attention, and hence were promptly deleted. It was always the intention of the sender that mattered, not the flying teddy bears greeting card that needed a complex software installation on my computer, requiring a shutdown and restart later. I didn't have time for all that! The baby didn't understand the concept of birthdays yet to gift me something. The husband was plain happy at the prospect of not having to exchange the present to the shop like last four of my birthdays. It had taken him four years to understand the hidden message behind, 'I love the watch, honey. This is exactly what I wanted. But I was just wondering if they had a different colour in this? Or perhaps, a different brand? Or a different shop maybe? That sold something…other…than…watches?'

Since now I was home, I had continued to nurse, which meant no wine and some whine to finish off my days with. Don't get me wrong, I loved being with my baby and would still do it all over again if I had to. But I would rather people stopped saying that I was on a 'break'—maternity break, but break nonetheless. Some even told me that I was on a long-term holiday. Holiday! Those blasphemous sons of guns! I strongly feel we should start one SAHM movement on Facebook to rename 'maternity break' to 'maternity 24x7 on-call duty without bathroom breaks' by burning nursing bras in public.

The naysayers (read, husbands or other non-parent people) are thinking that I am exaggerating. They are questioning how hard it can be to take care of a tiny, harmless person, who only has a few basic needs to be met after all. Of course if I compare the SAHM's job with that of a firefighter or a crab fisherman, it may fall short in the level of difficulty (although still not in terms of the number of hours you work). But it is definitely way more daunting than what the hubbies do or what the SAHMs like me once did in their corporate jobs.

Because in a corporate job, you sit down for starters.

You sit on a chair the whole day for heaven's sake and have coffee that has not been reheated three times and that doesn't have to be gulped down. Whereas, as a stay-at-home mom to a small child, you workout involuntarily the entire day, as dictated by your tiny yet relentless personal fitness trainer. The workout goes on something like this:

The pick-up-everything-from-the-floor-else-baby-will-put-it-in-his-mouth Leg Squat: At least 50 reps. All day long. Breathers allowed when your child naps. Speed and reflex action are key here. How quickly can you get down

to stop him from swallowing that fallen SIM card?
Variation: The squats can be accompanied with alternate arm stretches. For example, when the baby rolls his plastic balls under the couch and needs them back, right away.

The take-baby-up-in-the-air-and-bring-him-down-flying-superman Triceps Curl: At least 5 reps, 3 times a day. You can do more, if you are greedy for his giggles. You can do even more if you want him to stop crying. Caution needs to be taken to make sure he doesn't bump into any low-hanging lamps etc. The timing also needs to be correct here. This shouldn't be done right after he has had his food, unless you want that food back all over your face.
Variation: You can incline your arms to make your baby fly laterally, or bring him completely down to floor level and pick again. Making swooshing sounds is highly recommended for added fun here.

The take-baby-in-your-arms-and-sit-up-from-lying-down-flat Ab Crunch: This one is most effective at night. Number of reps vary, depending on how many times he wakes up in the night and needs rocking to go back to sleep, with a minimum of six. This one is reserved for the night on purpose when you are resting after a hard day's work, thinking that your workout for the day is done. It is only when you push yourself beyond your limits do you build those muscles in places you didn't even know existed in your body.
Variation: You can make your baby lie on your tummy and try patting him first. If he doesn't go back to sleep like that

(mine never did), you can sit up. The pressure of his weight on your tummy while sitting up will burn extra calories.

The stoop-over-baby's-cot-and-pat-his-bum-until-he-falls-asleep Forward Bend: This is done any time of the day or night, whenever the baby needs to sleep. This is more of a yogic posture for increased flexibility. So, it is not about the number of reps but about how long you can hold this pose. My back would generally give up after 15 minutes or so which could then only be healed by a serving of ice cream straight from the box. Never understood the logic behind this.

Variation: This can also be practiced while changing your baby's diaper, multiple times a day. The fact that he would wiggle like an octopus and keep sitting up while you do that makes it extra challenging.

The sit-baby-on-one-leg-and-stand-up-from-the-floor Quad Stretch: This one goes on the whole day long, especially when you try to sit down with him on the floor to relax and play. The baby will need to be picked up at that very moment. So you can bend one leg, place him on one thigh, and lift both of you up. Number of reps will be as much as the baby needs. You can keep alternating the leg each time if you get tired. Unfortunately you only have two.

Variation: Not much, except that while getting up, you can try to pick up the puffed rice that the baby had spilled on the floor earlier.

The carry-baby-in-one-arm-and-do-housework-with-the-other Pilates Body Balance: This one is practiced more regularly when the baby is still very small. Once he starts crawling, this needs to be done only in crisis situations. Like it is his lunch time and food is not ready. Or if he needs to grab that phone that you are talking to your boss on. Of course if he is crying, this exercise becomes the most important one until he settles enough for the Flying Superman Tricep Curl and both your arms are free.

Variation: The baby will be pulling your hair while you do this to make it harder for you. So with that single working hand, you will also need to free your hair from his clutches while stirring salt in the pan and meticulously keeping him away from the fire. It only sounds easy.

The lift-heavy-objects-that-you-always-asked-the-husband-to-help-you-with Weight Training: This can be done both indoors and outdoors with the baby. Outdoors can be in the form of toting a heavy-duty diaper bag that has enough supplies to last your baby a decade on a marooned island in the Caribbean. Or in the form of taking the car seat out with a baby sleeping in it and lugging it across the other end of the road since you couldn't find a parking spot nearby. While indoors, this can be done by moving baby's cot, high chairs, swings, etc., in and out of the storeroom according to how much he will use those things.

Variation: Seriously? Don't you think the above is already enough to wilt away your body and deserve a month-long massage?

The all-day-long-marathon Cardio Session: No workout is complete without this. There are different ways to work out a sweat with the baby around. You can dance to entertain him, bounce him in your lap or simply run after him as he crawls towards the dustbin when you are busy filing your nails. While outdoors with the baby you can get a good briskwalk or jog when the baby is done watching you shop at the supermarket and wants to get home immediately.
Variation: Many times the baby will enhance the challenge by refusing to sit in the stroller so you have to carry him back home while running and pushing the stroller all the way.

If you take all of the above and add other thankless jobs of cooking, de-cluttering and endless laundry, you will have a person who by evening needs the help of someone to ward a fly off her nose. And all that person did the whole day was to stay at home with the baby.

And it is not just about the physical stress. Not even half of it is about physical stress actually.

So, we normally hear people say they have to deal with a lot of shit at work. Shit like their bosses took credit for their work. Or shit like there is a lot of politics at work. Basically, anything that makes them unhappy at work is loosely termed as shit. Here's the kind of shit that moms who stay at home have to go through every day, multiple times a day and at multiple places—the REAL one. Many dirty diapers over. The fact that it is called poop in the baby world does not make it any cuter. It is so important in her life that it is a matter of a mini celebration when her baby finally goes after being stuck up for a couple of days. This is what her life comes down to. Then of course there are those fateful mornings when she has to clean it off her clothes or deal with her baby trying to pick it up and put it in his mouth. Talk about having a shitty day at work!

Nothing humanizes you more than seeing (and analysing) human faeces every day. This is possibly one thing that makes the relationship between your husband and you stronger in those first weeks of your child's birth. Families that share excretion stories together, live together. You might think of yourself as a la-di-da diva in your outside world swinging away a Fendi and strutting on a Manolo Blahnik all day for all your baby cares. But when it comes to his diaper, you have to swallow your pride, keep your breath in and get down to filthy business with your manicured hands. A few days into parenthood and you start discussing poop colour and consistency with anyone around you like you would discuss weather or politics. Fellow members (read, parents) of your poop appreciation society make no bones of it at all. Way before children are potty trained, they start making poop faces and giving signals that they are about to start the act. Even if they don't, nine times out of ten you can be certain that they are up to something if they look calm and mesmerized for more than a few minutes. Like Aristotle looking out of a window, thinking great ideas. They will behave like soft little kittens that haven't done anything and will continue with business as usual after they are done. It is hard to stomach that those babies are capable of such nuclear level explosions in their diapers with their golf ball sized tummies. (Sorry if that is a lot of graphic information for you, but were you really expecting to find pictures of the Taj Mahal in a book about babies and parenting?)

And now that we are on the topic of body fluids, we might as well pay due respect to the other members of this family—pee, spit, vomit, saliva, snot, boogers, to name a few—that your senses, clothes and body are subjected to on an hourly basis. I am not exaggerating here. At any given point of time when the baby is awake, he is either spitting after his meal, drooling from teething or pissing right at your face the moment you take his diaper off. Now of course those little monsters are worth every bit of that slime and there is nothing in this world you can't get used to, especially when it comes to your own child. But with Hubby gone away the whole day, I was the only one at the receiving end of those gross fluid squirts all the time, which I could have lived without.

At work, you have to bear with a lot of people with a smile on your face, even if you'd rather wish they were never born. However forced this socialization might be, you still get to engage in a minimum of one adult conversation per day. A conversation where you don't have to add an extra 'y' at the end of each word—'Where did the *fishy* go? Under your *legy*? To have some *milky*?' Where you don't always have to talk in interrogative and answer it yourself—'Who wants to have carrots for lunch? Me, me, me.' Where you don't have to fake excitement at something you know the other person will hate with a passion—'Look here baby, those are some amazing nose drops I am going to pour in your nostrils now!'

Monday at work sucks. Big time. But guess what? There is no concept of weekend for SAHM as all her days are exactly the same. She can't even get a sick day off. She can't fall sick at all, for that matter.

At least everyone else can sulk on Facebook and down three cups of coffee on a Monday morning, but the stay-at-home mom doesn't even have a reason for that. Oh the joy of whiling away time in office on Monday mornings, while reeling from the sloshed over weekends! Not in our calendars anymore. And did I say there is no chance for happy dancing on Fridays either?

Some other luxuries that you miss when you stay at home with your child:

- ☆ Being able to type *and* finish an entire email without little fingers tugging at you or your laptop.
- ☆ Getting an idea and thinking about it for as long as you want without getting interrupted by someone needing you immediately.
- ☆ Staring outside the window and doing nothing for more than 1 minute.
- ☆ Making a phone call, complete with pleasantries and goodbyes.
- ☆ Just simply stepping out of the building for fresh air and coming back whenever you want.
- ☆ Having a workspace that is always clean—one that is not even cleaned by you.

Your work boss or clients almost never go through belly cramps or other inexplicable problems that they can only communicate by crying. A baby does. Your boss and your clients can feed themselves. A baby can't. You don't have to stress out about anyone waking up from their naps before you have finished shaving your second underarm. You don't shave underarms at work anyway. You are not responsible for anyone bumping their heads or falling down from their chairs. If your boss gets sick, it is his problem, not yours.

Sprinkle all of it with constant feelings of unnecessary guilt and toss in daily sleep deprivation to the mix—that is a lot of stress to be living with. My office project deadlines suddenly look like a Disney cruise to me now.

A work environment is pretty controlled. The work is almost always defined in set modules with predictable end goals. One thing always leads to another. Parenting, on the other hand, defies all reason. As a stay-at-home mom, my day was rife with moments when the last strands of my sanity were pushed over the edge. When I would say out aloud to myself, 'But this doesn't make any sense at all!'

Following are my top insane parenting moments of all time:

(It was a tough judgment, considering the 24x7 circus that went on in the house, but I have tried my best to pick the ones that were most annoying and occurred most frequently.)

☆ Your baby is happily sitting on the floor playing with his toys for once. The sun is smiling, the birds are chirping and the world generally seems to be at peace. Which is when you decide to push your luck further and go take a quick shower. Half a minute of continued peace later you are confidently pouring soap in your hands and you hear repetitive screams. Soaking wet, you make a dash out of the bathroom praying that a dingo didn't just climb up your house through the balcony and ate your baby. But the only thing you find changed between your pre- and post-shower world are the coordinates of a certain plastic rattle, which is now under the couch and hence no longer in the reach of the tiny hands, turning your baby's entire world upside down.

☆ Once again it is a sunny day and the birds are chirping. Your baby is fed, bathed, diaper changed and generally happy. You take two hours to get dressed, bundle the baby up and pack copious amount of baby food—enough to feed the entire Spartan army for a week. You strap him in the car seat and are just about to start the car. While adjusting the rear view mirror, you smell something dubious. Yes, the baby's pooped again and will keep resisting getting changed. The sun is going down and so is your will to un-bundle, bundle and wrestle your child back into the car seat.

☆ Your baby is throwing a tantrum for something, and you for once know what he is asking for. It is one of those words he speaks clearly, like apple or cheese. You, in all your sincerity and a desperate need for approval from him, hand the damn thing to him. He still keeps on throwing a tantrum for the exact same thing. IT IS RIGHT THERE IN YOUR HAND, KID!

☆ Your baby very enthusiastically announces that he wants to sleep. Two hours have passed since then and you are still shut in a dark room with him, imagining how life would be in a house where children meant what they said. You have lost any will to live by this point. And then fortune smiles on you and little eyes begin to close. Right at that moment, the Fisher Price musical sea horse buried under a mountain of laundry starts beeping, making your baby more awake than ever. (You may want to note here that this is the same toy that had stopped working a week before when your baby had really wanted to play with it.)

Yes, none of it makes sense. I have come to realize that parenting is not logical but biological. (Whatever that means, just want to stress that it is not logical.)

While working at my corporate job, I often felt that my job was very monotonous—working on that same excel sheet for hours, until I had to read my son's favourite book twelve times in a day with the same level of novelty each time. You sometimes think you should quit your job because they didn't promote you to the next level. How about being in a job that has no levels at all? A mom is a mom forever. She never gets promoted to senior director mom or vice president mom. You cringe at having to take the burden of someone else's work while he is on vacation. Here your child is on a lifelong holiday and you have to do all his work. You think you are not paid enough at your job. Well, hello? A stay-at-home mom doesn't get paid at all. (Yes, she is paid in pure love and all that, but getting some cash never hurts.)

I could go on, but I think I have made my case here. I am not asking for any medals of bravery for staying at home with my baby. Or maybe just one for the days he ate his broccoli. I did not do any sacrifice that needs to be glorified—except of course, to the husband. (You tell me you had a tough day at work, dear Hubby and I'll up the game with a baby that refused to get off my shoulder the entire day.)

All I am saying is that staying at home with my son helped me gain a different, and perhaps a better perspective on things. It also made me realize how I could have traumatized my own parents once. If I were them, I would have never bought me a scooter on my eighteenth birthday.

I have never had a more demanding boss than my son in over a decade of my corporate experience. I haven't done any job that was more difficult than this job. And yet, my job as a stay-at-home mom has been the only one where I looked forward to waking up every single morning.

Ridiculously early. Every single darned morning.

Seriously, when do the little ones start sleeping in till late?

(What? I know I chose to have this baby and love him more than my life. But a mommy can still rant, all right?)

Does It Get Easier?
No, You Get Better at It

I think I need to cut these babies some slack here. They do turn your world upside down and break your back a million times during the day, but the ups of parenting definitely overweigh the downs. Right when you think it is impossible to love those little devils anymore, they do the cuddliest of things to release truckloads of oxytocin in your body and make you swoon. But those babies can do you more good than that! Research suggests that a happy baby can do wonders to enhance your own creativity levels, for example. About nine months into the game, and I could draw a list of at least nine more functional benefits of babies. (Perhaps by now you are thinking that I have a secret partnership with the cosmic ministry of reproduction and my sole job is to evangelize the world about procreating. But trust me, I don't. Although I'd be excellent at that job.)

Here goes.

- ☆ You can easily blame your burps and farts on those babies. To cover up more, just say something before anyone has noticed. 'What is that smell? Was that you, dirty baby? Yes, it was you!' And laugh away. Babies would never protest and may just join in the fun without realizing the joke is on them.
- ☆ You don't have to clean your house anymore. Because your little ones still live there and cleaning with them around is like brushing your teeth while still eating chocolate. Totally pointless. Always overrated. (Many times I have let my son spill things on the floor, even when I knew he was doing that; but I just wanted some moments of peace.)
- ☆ If you do want to clean the house, you can put all that clutter in less obvious places and again blame it on your babies. Later when you find dried-up orange peels inside your pillowcase, just act nonchalant and ask them why they did that. Works every time.
- ☆ Babies can stop traffic and have people hold the door for you. I have had nice people lifting up my stroller with baby in it and putting it in the train while I warmed my hands over a disposable coffee cup and gossiped on the phone. Next thing I want to try is to pull a sullen face and say something to the tune of, 'Babies, sigh! They are a lot of work. I haven't slept in ages and didn't get a chance to have my breakfast this morning, you know,' in the hope

that someone will offer me their seat and/or their packet of potato chips.

☆ You can use babies as an excuse for your general sloppiness and carelessness. They are almost always going through some developmental stage which can make your life harder than it is. Teething is a great one. You can get away with murder by saying that your baby is teething.

☆ Babies are great for your self-esteem. Hide a candy under a pillow, exclaim when you take it out after a few seconds and voila! You are the biggest magician that was ever born on this planet. You may be like the least important person at the job you hate to go to everyday, but you can always turn to your baby and tell yourself what a bloody awesome person you are to have created a marvel like that. You are their superhero, funniest cartoon and favourite singer rolled into one. Clueless babies can't even make out if you sing the same song over and over again and get the tune and lyrics wrong every time.

☆ Babies serve as a fantastic reason for retail therapy. There is always something to shop for them in bright, cheerful colours. Since they are naturally cute, they will look good in any clothes you buy for them. So you don't have to stress out on their cellulite showing or their clothes not coordinating or coordinating too much with their shoes or bags.

☆ You can finally be yourself and indulge in senseless silly talks whenever you want. Your kids want the real mommy, not the fake-smiling-with-a-co-worker-she-hates mommy or the politically-correct-carefully-watching-her-words-at-networking-parties mommy.

☆ Being allowed to 'help' with household chores is a game for them when they are a little older. My son loves to load the washing machine, picking each piece of cloth gently one by one and tossing it completely in. Then pressing all the buttons he can get his hands on. By having him do that I not only give him the equivalent of a trip to Disneyland in terms of wow factor, but I also get to sit for a few minutes and crack my knuckles. I can safely bank on this until he gets big enough to visit the *real* Disneyland for himself and refuses to do anything that doesn't offer that level of excitement.

So by now there had been nine whole months (and counting) of my son's utter dependence on my husband and me, of us running around him, of endless dinner take outs, of not finding time for anything, of reaching late everywhere, of two-day-old dirty dishes in the kitchen, of waiting things to get better and yet not wanting the moments to pass, of pulling hair in frustration and laughing it all off.

Of an incomparable pride at strangers ogling at him. Of extreme outbursts of unadulterated, selfless love. Of constant, downright happiness.

We were getting a hang of it all now, although the husband had just finished a parenting IQ test on the internet with a measly score of 54 per cent. But since he was the self-proclaimed sleeping baby expert in the house now, we let him off the hook. The boys did give me a few hours of peace on weekend afternoons, when they slept hugging each other on the couch with ESPN playing in the background.

'You have to start training them early on real men's ways of life,' Husband whispered to me as he snuggled with baby on the couch.

'Sure, what is the next lesson in that series? Burping the alphabet?' I asked.

'The way he is going; he will learn that in no time. So proud of my champ!'

'Please spare him the lesson on complimenting women, will you?'

'Say, why?'

'Yesterday when I wore my new top that I thought I looked awesome in, what was the first thing you said?'

'What did I say?'

'That I should not buy clothes with horizontal stripes—even when I have lost a lot of my pregnancy weight.'

'So, should I not be honest with you? I mean, of course you looked great in that. You look good in everything you wear.'

'Don't bother; it's too late for that now. By the way, our son definitely seems to be doing great in the laziness department. He was late to be born, was late to start crawling and will sure be late to walk. Not that I am concerned, but just drawing some parallels with your lifestyle there.'

'Thank you. Will you now stop berating me when I tell you I will be back in a jiffy and that jiffy sometimes means a couple of hours? Do you understand it all now? We men do things at our own pace. Doing everything on time is such a waste of time.'

'Er...like how?'

'I will explain that to you later.'

'What is that one thing you will ever do now? Did you put those suitcases back in the attic?'

'If I told you I would do something, I *will* do it. There is no need to remind me of it every month. By the way, our son is doing great in the vocal department too. He has already uttered his first word and his screams can put a woman-petrified-on-seeing-a-cockroach to shame. So there, he does take after you in some respects too.'

'Oh he takes after me in many more ways than that, all right. Intelligence, for example.'

'That is not possible. Of course that is all because of me.'

'There is evidence to show that the genes that determine intelligence are all in the X chromosome—which boys inherit completely from their mothers. Unlike girls, who inherit from both their parents.'

'Oh, that is all nonsense.'

'Well, I just hope our son doesn't take the "not agreeing to anything" gene from you. Anyway, the first word that our son spoke, albeit very early, is not mama. Not even anything close to "mum". His first word—that I am not very happy to admit—was "ball".'

'Bwahahaha. We do need a fast bowler in our team.'

'And if it is already possible, he hates shopping and going to malls in general. The sight of clothes stacked tightly in hangers always upsets him. I haven't been able to do any real shopping with him at all, and he is just a baby if you come to think of it!'

'Thank god for answered prayers. You already have enough clothes and you still say you have nothing to wear. Baby would never say anything like that. Right my *gobbledygooksugarcandyhubbanumrollypolly* baby?'

'Oh, come on now. My saying "I have nothing to wear" is similar to your saying "there is nothing to eat at home", even when the fridge is stocked. It just means that I don't have what I want to wear at that point in time.'

'Baby, do you understand what Mama is saying? No, right? Mama, please let both of us sleep now.'

So by now my son was starting to get a personality, and if the above conversation is any measure, he was turning into a real boy. There must have been a good amount of prenatal testosterone transfer in our case. When they are little, babies are just babies—not boys or girls. We do dress them appropriately to make their gender very clear to the world. But other than that, there is no difference really. During pregnancy, whenever someone asked me if I wished for a boy or a girl, I could never answer that question. I wanted a baby that smelled like one and looked like one. That's it. Perhaps I was blissfully forgetting that the baby would grow up to be a man or a woman one day, and hence I should have a clear preference of one over the other. But I still don't have one. I can't say if I miss making frilly tutus now that I have a boy, or if I'd miss buying socks with tiny automobile prints on them if I had a girl.

The other day when he was playing with Hubby's electric shaver, I shuddered to think that my son will start using one in a few years. His pinky white skin, smooth enough to trickle down a blob of butter, will have hair emerging all over. MY BABY WILL HAVE ARMPIT HAIR! He will sweat and stink after a round of sports. He will grow up with an obsession of transformers or other such machinated character movies that I can never survive without a continuous supply of sugary snacks and a game of scrabble, secretly played on my phone.

His cheeks that look perpetually stuffed with cotton candy—that magically gives them a crimson colour on the outside—will deflate. His voice will crack. He will refuse to ask for driving directions from someone and may even forget to put the toilet seat down. He will terribly suck at multitasking. At the age of two, he doesn't differentiate between girl things and boy things. He probably doesn't even know that there are two genders. He likes to wear my heels and pretend play with my make-up as much as he likes to try his daddy's shirts on. But when he grows up, he will hate to be associated with anything feminine that has a slight tendency to dilute his machismo. Men are very territorial that way. Women on the other hand, despite their full-time job of being incredibly awesome, are more accepting and open to take on men's ways if need be. It is easy as pie for the women.

Today, if I look around my house, my son's footprints are there in every nook and cranny. There is a little blue shoe that I keep tripping over. When I sit in the bathtub,

I hear the squeak of a rubber ducky under me. There is a half-eaten banana smeared on my carpet and my bed has jumping dolphins stickered on them. The kitchen has motely plastic blocks scattered on the floor. My coat pockets have opened packets and wrappers of his snacks that I carry for him when we go outdoors and he refuses to eat. Among my hardbound books about the meaning of life and how to lose pregnancy weight, there is a rather hungry caterpillar book peeping out to be noticed from the bookshelf. A tiny sock always shows up entwined in my washed up laundry that was diligently separated from his clothes.

My baby lives inside me. Wherever I go, a little bit of him always comes with me. All the times he fell asleep on my shoulder, I hugged him tight as if to not let go. It was almost like the world came to a standstill at that moment. Even the airplanes seemed to stop flying and birds didn't chirp, as if because their little bystander wasn't there to wave at them anymore. My whole world muzzled down in the sound of a balmy lullaby played on repeat in his room. At that very moment, I felt that there wasn't a place I'd rather be or a thing I'd rather do—but to smell him, smell of him and become him!

It is difficult to imagine that he will grow up into an adult, a man at that too. A man who will stand taller than me and will guide me to all things new. A man who will not like my interruptions and will object when I forbid him from something. A man who may not like if I kiss him in public. I won't have an answer to all his whys and he may feel I just don't get what he says. But for me he will still be my baby, even beyond his 40th birthday. A little bit of him will always come with me wherever I go.

Cut back again to nine months, when my son was a lot more fun to be with than ever before. The belly laughs were more frequent and his exploratory sense was getting more enhanced—much to my trouble. There were newer challenges to cope with now. Bathing him, for example. During his first months, bathing him was an art of extreme meticulousness for me, almost like jugglery, as he couldn't even keep his neck up for crying out loud. So, by keeping one hand behind his neck, he had to be immersed in the water, and soaped, wiped, scrubbed with the other. There was this constant fear of drowning him if he got too slippery. The husband was still to muster up the courage to give him a bath. No one could talk to me when I bathed the baby lest I should lose concentration. My shoulders were tensed up all the time. Needless to say, my son was in and out of the bath in 3 minutes flat and that first baby soap bottle that we had bought was still half full even after nine months. I used to bathe him in a Winnie-the-pooh baby tub that I would fill with water and place on our dining table with all living room lights on, as the cramped bathroom was too risky.

But at nine months, since he could move, sit and stand a little, I moved him to the adult bathtub with shower in our bathroom. And that was the problem that he could move, sit and stand a little. Because that is what he did during the bath as well. And while at it, he would bump his head into the faucets, spray everywhere with the shower and drink from that remaining soap bottle when I wasn't looking. And he never wanted that bath to end. It has been getting worse since then. Hell hath no fury like a child who has been asked to get out of the bathtub.

Total time taken to bathe an older baby = More than when he is younger. Difficulty = Still the same.

Hang in there, dear parent.

Now feeding him should have become better, as he had started eating a lot of adult food, you'd think? Not exactly. So earlier he used to feed for hours getting zonked out in between his meals and up and hungry again in no time. But now he sat on his own chair and ate with a spoon that he insisted on holding by himself to spill all food on the floor, still taking hours to finish the whole activity. He was particularly interested in eating stuff off the floor, it gave him a feeling that he had hunted for it and earned it. I am pretty sure that even today, half of his daily calorie intake comes from pieces of dried up food he discovers stuck in his high chair from days before. As an infant, he knew only one taste—of lukewarm, sweet milk. But now he had a more sensitive palate and he became quite predictably unpredictable with what he liked. Something that he relished one day, he would refuse to eat a second morsel of on the next, leaving me in a crisis situation of not having anything else ready for him. For all such instances we had yogurt in our house that he always liked. But, on Sunday evenings we would run out of that too and all hell would break loose.

Total time taken to feed an older baby = Slightly lesser than when he is little. Difficulty = Almost the same.

Keep calm and carry on parenting.

During his first months, my son didn't do much during his free time. He just lay flat, cooed occasionally, stared at the ceiling and secretly laughed at people making idiotic baby conversations with him—thank god he couldn't record them and share on the internet. So he didn't need much to stay entertained and he didn't even offer much in return. But now that he offered a hell lot more, he also demanded much more, that little business tycoon. The average duration a toy could keep him engaged at this age was 0.5 seconds and it hasn't improved since then. But if he did like something, he liked it with all his passion and you couldn't take it away from him. And that happened only with things that you couldn't bring home, like those kiddie rides in the mall.

Total time taken to entertain an older baby = Much more than ever before. Difficulty = Way more.

You have no choice now, dear parent. Parenting was always a one-way ticket.

He used to take two or three naps during the day, but now he was down to one. At the age of two, he sometimes even goes without one, which tells me he is ready for a full-time job. As a smaller baby, whatever little he slept during the nights, he just slept and did nothing else. As he became older, he developed a keen interest in horizontal acrobatics during sleep. I have woken up on more nights than you'd imagine to lay my hand on him, only to jump from my bed to not find him there, but at the diametrically opposite end of the bed. This not-letting-parents-sleep pact of kids continues even until their teenage years and beyond, when you stay up waiting for them to return from their late night college parties. At any given time when I shared my bed with him, I was entitled to less than 5 per cent of the total available bed space for both of us. If I dared to protest, he would climb over my neck and continue to sleep there. For the number of times I have woken up with swollen lips and black eyes, thanks to his punches and kicks, I strongly feel we need to have a parental abuse helpline in place.

Total time an older baby sleeps during 24 hours = Lesser than he did as an infant. Difficulty to put him to sleep = Still the same – The hour-long rocking sessions are only replaced by equally long verbal negotiation sessions to convince them to go to bed.

Don't worry; parenting is tough only for the first forty years.

In short, this baby business is a lost battle—for the parents, I mean. Everyone tells new parents, 'It gets easier with time and this too shall pass.' Yes it passes, like everything does, thanks. But no, it does not get easier, it only gets differently difficult. And that is so not the same as easy. Parenting is like a 'megathlon'—you finish one challenge and you are up for the next one, except that this 'megathlon' runs for your entire life. If it was colic yesterday, it is temper tantrums today and it will be teenage girlfriend problem tomorrow.

The good news is that your children are always worth it all at the end of the day.

(When they are finally in bed.)

Meet the New Me, Who Is Nothing Short of Awesome (At Least While the Baby Sleeps)

About a month shy from his first birthday, my son was turning more and more into a superbaby—a baby, but with traits similar to Superman. He didn't wear underwear over his pants, or any underwear at all for that matter. But he had tamed a lion and a mouse at the back of his diaper, which often appeared from above his pajamas when he crawled or stood up. His boundless levels of energy, charged up by a living, milk-powered battery, matched those of the energizer bunny. He had mystical healing powers and could *un*-suck a bad day by his gummy smile. He could also heal his own booboos through a dosage of kisses from me and by being allowed to drop valuable objects on floor.

He had a microscopic vision and could hunt down the tiniest of objects that even a vacuum cleaner could not catch. The more dangerous the object, the better was his vision. His antics offered complete entertainment free of cost for all age groups. He was multifaceted—both, a time machine who took us back to our childhood and the future bestselling author of *How to always bow down to your boss and be happy about it*. He was my sun and moon rolled into one. Sun, because he woke me up and moon, because he stayed up at night like a watchman to regularly check if the world around him was still in order. Moms of little boys indeed work from son up till son down.

Superbaby was mighty strong for his age. Sometimes while I was still carrying him, he'd spot something interesting on the floor and make a dive right through my arms, head first. He wasn't scared of anything except a pressure cooker whistle. He was extremely fast for his age too, or that of mine for that matter. He had bat ears and was able to hear sounds like the creaky door opening or a keyboard clicking from the other end of the house. I, on the other hand, had gone half deaf by then, thanks to his piercing shrieks darted right into my ear drums.

At eleven months, even a pack of Gouda cheese in my fridge was older than him—my son was so little and yet so influential. If some trivial thing cracked him up, Hubby and I would do that over and again to hear his cackling laughter. He called the shots in our family like a ringmaster, and will continue to do so for the rest of our lives. People did the silliest of activities to woo him, just for a chance to hold him for a second, but he would never even care two hoots and carry on with his own business—he truly was my superbaby.

I had grown a lot too, and not talking just about my

waistline here—the bulging tyre of which had made my politically incorrect cleaner ask me if there was another baby cooking in there. If there is a sure-shot way to make a woman feel awful, it is none other than calling her pregnant when there is definitely not a chance in the world that she could be. 'If you eat muffins every day to alleviate stress, you will grow muffins on you,' was my answer to him.

But his snide remark made me think of that time, years before my pregnancy era, when a rather chunky colleague at work had told me that she was pregnant, and that too already for five months then. My immediate reaction to her was that her bump didn't show at all, as she always had such a huge belly anyway—not that I told her that last part. Other women would normally consider such a thing as a compliment. I, for instance, had happily endured a root canal treatment from my dentist simply because he had told me I didn't look pregnant at four months. But my colleague had clearly taken offence at my response to her, even when I hadn't meant it entirely. My karma had come around in the form of my cleaner that morning.

So anyway, back to the point that it was not just my body that had become bigger in every direction due to the baby, it was also my person that had gone under an amazing metamorphosis. It is said that the moment a child is born, the mother is also born. But the two births (of mom and baby) are a sea different. For a child, the birth is a transition from 0 to 1, from a state of oblivion to existence. For me, it was from 1 to 2, or 6—as I had suddenly become this totally new person who was doing everything differently. The change hit me so fast and from all directions that I didn't even get a chance to realize what just happened. Over the next few months, I just kept on going with the flow, congratulating myself for getting through yet another day of not turning into a certified psychotic.

I was so immersed in my own fantasy world of looking for baby solid food recipes online and singing nursery rhymes in the shower all by myself—that my time before mommyhood seemed to me like a past life or a fiction book I had once read that did not have pages chewed up by my son. It was only when other non-mommy people pointed out, did I realize that the things I was doing then as second nature and still continue to do are not considered normal by the general human race—things that apparently one would only do as a mom.

Things like:

☆ Pointing out and saying, 'Look doggy!,' 'Look birdie!,' 'Look at that Old Macdonald's cow!', whenever I take my son out. If I could get money for every time that happens, I'd probably be able to buy out Old MacDonald and his entire farm, and rename the rhyme after me. Take the baby out of the picture and I will look like a colossal idiot pointing to things and getting excited on my own—I have been through that a few times too. I may also confess that I have the crane guilt—the feeling you get when you spot a *biiiig crane* on the road and your child is not with you to see it.

- ☆ Having a handbag that is always exploding with my son's food stuff, backup food stuff and emergency food stuff in case he throws a tantrum in the mall. A bag that is full of cookie crumbs deep down in the pockets that never go away and will turn into rare fossils one day. The laptop that has stayed long enough in the bag also has its USB slots full of crumbs. And a car that is perpetually stuffed with snack items placed strategically for a snappy handover to a screaming child at the back.
- ☆ Catching my son's chewed up, unwanted food in my hand—the one that took me a whole morning of I-can't-feed-my-baby-processed-food guilt to cook and pack in that handbag. Sometimes even allowing him to spit in my hand when I can't get that god forsaken napkin out of the bag.
- ☆ Cleaning dried up yogurt stains and such from his face with my own spit. (People can forget to carry water and they run out of wet wipes sometimes.)
- ☆ If I haven't figured it out by any other way, sniffing my son's bum to check for poop signs in public. Go on, let out a loud scream of 'Ewwwwww', you non-mommy people, while admiring your-flat-as-a-pancake tummy in the mirror. But that is the only foolproof and hands-off method to perform this very crucial task.
- ☆ Bringing baby 5 minutes into any random conversation with any one, once even with a random stranger asking for directions, something like the following:

'I am looking for the public library here, can you help me?' Random Stranger asks me.

'Sure. Just go straight for two blocks and take a left towards the shopping mall. You will find it right at the corner.'

'There is a shopping mall close by? Sorry, I am new here.'

'Yes, a very good one and it has a lot of fun activities for kids too. My son loves the indoor swing there. Here's a funny story: Once I took him to the mall, thinking I'd be back in a few minutes while he slept in the stroller. But he woke up immediately as we entered and started pointing towards the swing. Can you believe it? It was the most amazing thing that happened with me that day!'

'Wow! It must be great to see your child do things like that.'

'Er, you don't have kids, do you?'

'No.'

'Okay then—I don't think we can be friends,' I thought to myself.

☆ Going out for a break and wanting to get back to the baby quickly, looking at his pictures even when he is around, spending all the effort in putting him to sleep and then missing him when he finally does. MAKE UP YOUR MIND ABOUT WHAT YOU WANT, WOMAN!

☆ Engaging in either super fast or super slow activities. There has been no normal pace here. It is either:

'Mom-stopthecar-takemehome-givememybottle-putmetosleep' in 5 minutes flat. Or: 'Waaaatchh meeee opeeen aaand cloooose thhhee doooor agaaaiiin agaaaaaiiiin aaaaaand agaaaaiiin becauuuuse I fiiiind thaaat funnnnyyyy'. Yawwwwn.

☆ Not giving a damn about the world.

'I don't care Mr Interviewer if you still have more questions left. My baby wants my phone right now; you can give the job to someone else'—something similar was my response to a recruiter who had called me for a phone interview while I was still not decided if I'd go back to work. Now I had scheduled that interview well, exactly at the time my baby napped during the day when I took him out for a stroll. But like all other situational ironies that are characteristic of small children, my son obviously decided to not sleep at that very moment and throw a fit instead. I tried my best to stay calm, as much as I could, what with wheeling the stroller with one hand, running fast to get to a place my son might like and panting through answers about my strengths and weaknesses. The recruiter had said he would take only 10 minutes and went on for 45. The baby wasn't willing to give up either. So in the end I had to. Of course the recruiter never called back. Baby and I had a good laugh about it just before he went to sleep—which was exactly 1 minute after I hung up the phone on the interviewer. Because, obviously it was time for him to sleep then.

☆ Celebrating the most trivial of things.
'He ate a quarter slice of cheese today and loved it!'
'He picked a peanut with his own two fingers! Yay, pop the bubbly!'
And stressing out at even more trivial things.
'What if I get a haircut and my baby doesn't recognize me?'

☆ Absolutely not tolerating anyone causing even a wee bit of discomfort to the baby.
'Your bunch of carrots just brushed against my baby.'
'Oh, I am sorry,' the fellow grocery-shopper replied.
'Hmm,' and I gave him the look that could pierce through his bald head.
'It's not like I did it intentionally,' he snapped at me.
'So you are saying that *we* were blocking your way with just our stroller, a baby trying to stand in it and a mom with groceries and diaper bag lugging onto her?'
'I already said sorry, didn't I? Why were you staring at me like I did something really bad?'
'If you have children, you'd know why I was doing that.'
'You are not the first mother in this world.'
'But I am the first and only mother to my baby. Now get out of my way!'

My own jaw dropped at what I just said, since I used to be quite a pushover earlier, who would buy something from a salesman even when she didn't want it just because she couldn't say no.

Not only was I doing completely new activities, but also my mind was a totally new animal now that I was a mom. I am sure that while I was zonked out in the hospital under the effect of epidural, they did a brain transplant on me. I had gone to the hospital with a normal brain that could half-finish crosswords before turning to page three of the newspaper. But what I came back with was a 'mommy-brain' that bordered on ADHD (Attention Deficit Hyperactivity Disorder) and had lost any cells that were responsible for remembering things. Things like, 'When I thought I'd brush my teeth, did I actually do it or I still have to?' or like, 'It's been an hour and water has still not boiled. Is it because the proverbial pot is actually being watched? Wait, I never turned the gas on!' or like, 'What is the name of this guy I am holding the visiting card of?'

When you are working your mind overtime, constantly worrying and planning, it is only natural that it will wear out at some point. A few minutes into my mommy-brain would read something like this:

Glad the baby is finally sleeping in his room. Let me rest my head for a few minutes on the couch before I go to steam vegetables for his lunch. But if I fall asleep, I will lose track of time and the baby might wake up even before the vegetables are ready. Maybe I should just lie down and check my phone for messages. Sister-in-law had called. It is also her birthday this month on the 5th. Or was it the 15th? 25th? I do remember the date ended with a 5. I have always been the first one to wish her on her birthday. I will find out as we still have time; August has only just started. Holy smoke! We are already in August? Still 2012, though. I am thirty-one and I have done nothing with my life. Thank god for this baby, at least now I have a reason to do more 'nothings' with my life, so cute he looks! Wait, baby had to get his vaccination done in August, or was it July? Dear god, I hope it was August. I must call the doctor to set up his vaccination appointment. Where in god's name is the phone when you need it? Oh it is right there in my hand. But the doctor is there only on Tuesday evenings; on all other days he sits at a place far away from home. What is the day today? I remember there was a Sunday a few days back when Hubby was home and I had put conditioner in my hair. That conditioner made my hair so rough. Which one was it? Head and Shoulders? I better stick to my good old L'Oréal. I must make a note of buying one when I go out with baby to the doctor's. I wonder if the baby has any sense of smell yet. The Head and Shoulders one did smell pretty strongly. Is that why he got upset when I picked him up right after my shower? God knows what goes on in their diminutive heads. I was going to do something, what was it? With the phone? Oh yes, call the doctor. It has definitely been two or even more days since Sunday, so it is not a Tuesday today. But I can always go another day of the week. I will need to drive down then. What time should I go? After his morning nap when he is playing? But he always poops then. I will need to carry all his sanitation paraphernalia with me. I can wait and go after that. But sometimes he takes a while and it is almost time for his next feed and nap. I can't keep waiting. Damn, why is this so difficult? Or perhaps I should go in the evening. Will it be too cold then? But he will be in the car and I can bundle him up well. So, evening it is. I need to fix the car seat then. I hope he doesn't get scared to sit in it like last time. They should probably make car seats more like baby beds. But they will need bigger cars for that, even trucks. Gosh! that will almost look like an ambulance. The thought scares me. My baby in an ambulance! Why do all these negative thoughts always creep in my head? I need to start meditating. But where is the time? Bloody hell, I am so tired, I already want to take a nap tomorrow. Time, yes. I need to get back home from the doctor's before 6 for Baby's bath and bedtime routine, otherwise he won't sleep easily. I will need to leave at 4 then. I must check the weather forecast. The last time I took him out it started raining and he got a cold. Or perhaps that was from yogurt? I haven't washed his bibs from then. Oh how I love those 30 minutes in the day when my laundry basket is empty, before my son wakes up and gets his clothes dirty again! When can I start washing his clothes with mine? It is such a waste to run the washing machine with three bibs and four pairs of his capsule-sized socks, half of which are always sucked by the machine. Wonder when they will make a machine that also folds laundry and puts it in the wardrobe. Is this the Stone Age or what? I should perhaps buy more clothes for him and another pack of baby-friendly detergent. So

> *that's quite a shopping list for today. I hope I remember to take the list with me when I go, unlike the last time when I bought two kilo oranges, in place of onions. And we already had oranges at home. Perhaps I will also get a juicer to pulp them all now. But wait, I have no space left in the kitchen. Let me do some work in the kitchen. Should I close all the doors, else the baby might wake up from the rattling of pots and pans? But if I close I may not be able to hear him at all. I haven't heard him for some time. Is he all right? God, I hope he is all right. Yes he is. Thank heavens! So what was I going to do with the phone? Call someone? Where did I put it again?*

I had read somewhere that a woman's mind is like an internet browser with multiple windows open all the time. I came to agree even more with this when I became a mom. My mind, when not attending to baby activities, was like a beehive with millions of thoughts buzzing in all directions, day or night. Come to think of it, it is not just the baby that causes you sleep deprivation. It is also all those times when that poor baby is sleeping but you are having troubles shutting your brain. Often at unearthly hours, I used to be up, evaluating myself as a mother or pondering over all the bad decisions I had ever taken during my life. Obviously 3 a.m. seemed to be the best time to log onto the internet to also learn about the Sudden Infant Death Syndrome and panic your heart out. My son's warm clothes also needed to be bought online right then, since winter was around the corner and oh my goodness, he didn't even have a good enough jacket to go out in.

Motherhood consumes a lot of your mind space, despite the activities associated with it being completely mindless. As a result you end up with a dysfunctional brain. Not that I wasn't forgetful in my pre-baby life, but now I was way worse and had the best excuse in the world to be like that. Once at a friend's house, I saw a pair of scissors lying on a coffee table which was quite low and hence easily reachable by small children. I immediately picked up the scissors and asked for it to be put away, only to realize later that there was no kid in that house, not even my own! More often than not I have tried to look for child safety toilet seat locks in public bathrooms, and reminded myself that it is not my house and my son can't sneak in here—my mind lives under such a constant fear all the time.

Just getting out of the house with a small child is also a rigorous mental exercise in itself.

'Have I taken everything? Bag, phone, water, food, house keys…'

<Baby starts to cry>

'Let me give him some water first.'

'So bag, phone, water, food, house keys, car keys, sunglasses…'

<Baby wants you again>

'Wait a second, baby, you want a biscuit? But I was packing it to give it to you on the way!'

'Okay, okay, here. Have one before we go.'

'So bag, phone, water, food, house keys, car keys, sunglasses, hand sanitizer…'

\<Baby tries to get up from the stroller\>
'Hang on there, you will fall down!'

'So bag, phone, water, food, house keys, car keys, sunglasses, hand sanitizer, baby's hat, jacket, umbrella…what else am I forgetting?'

\<Baby cries again\>

'Oh, the baby of course! Mama is not going to forget you my sugar cup!'

'So we are good to go now. I wish I were an octopus with that many hands to carry everything. Or legs? Whatever.'

'My legs, my feet feel weird. Damn, I forgot to put shoes on!'

I keep everything aside and lace my shoes up. Baby is impatient to get out at any cost now. So in all hurry I forget the umbrella on the table next to my shoe rack. And while soaking wet in the rain, I remember the time when I could just get into the car and go wherever I wanted, whenever I wanted.

Motherhood did bring a big change in my attitude as well, however. For good. My son turned out to be my very own spiritual master, teaching me the art of living every day. We read so much literature and follow so many gurus to learn how to live life well, when the fountainhead of life's wisdom is right there in our laps.

I am not being sarcastic when I say that.

A child is perfect in all sense when he is born. He has no prejudices or pretensions. He is not bothered by what is happening around him; he is completely in tune with his own self. He is the epitome of living in the moment—which is the crux of all spiritual teachings. He is just content to be and not become anything. He is totally at peace with his existence—not wanting to be at some other place or in some other time. He asks what he wants, and is happy when he gets it. If he doesn't, then he expresses his concern loud and clear, and moves on pretty quickly. He holds no grudges against anyone. He laughs heartily when something tickles him. He is innocent and curious, without a care for tomorrow. He lives life to the fullest, eats to his heart's content and does what he likes. He means no harm to anyone, at least not intentionally. He lives and lets others live. He loves and likes to be loved, sans any crazy expectations. And that's just how he rolls. The funny thing is that we are all born like that, but then we forget it over the years as we run fast to grow up and reach our respective finishing lines.

My therapeutic baby, as I like to call him, has given me such important lessons of life, that no book could ever give. His life was like a bonsai version of my own that I could see up close like a giant and fix everything that was going wrong with it. I could never do that with my own life which was a mere miniscule part of an unfathomable grandeur that surrounded me. His broken plastic car needed only a screwdriver to fix. His dismantled tower of blocks could be erected again by me in a few minutes. His lion and crocodile were not scary. His jellyfish didn't sting. His fabric house needed no locks. His radio never played a sad song. His happiness lay in pushing the elevator buttons. His day was made on seeing two cats in a row. His pretend pans always had delicious food in them. His gun did not kill anyone, it blew soap bubbles.

His world made me fall in love with mine all over again. I started to find positivity everywhere, as I wanted to transmit that positivity to my son. I wanted him to believe that he could wave goodbye to the moon and that if he clapped, puppies came out of their dens. Somewhere deep down, I believed or at least wanted to believe, it all to be true as well.

Before baby I used to sweat the small stuff out. Stuff like lamenting over what someone said to me or agonizing over why a friend didn't return my call. With the baby I was running around his clock, meeting his demands and entertaining him like a clown for 24 hours a day. I only got a few breathers here and there. I learnt to use that time to relax and dig into a sinful piece of chocolate, rather than thinking about the non-issues of life. I realized that my baby's problems, that he could not even communicate, were way bigger than mine. While my worries used to be about bad performance review at work, his agonies were about teeth trying to push through tiny gums that hurt. Many times I complained about feeling out of place at some gathering I had to be a part of, and here my baby had to deal with feeling out of place in this new world outside my womb.

For once, I was not the focus of my life, my son was—something that felt like a breath of fresh air after years of suffocating self-involvement. It was about putting another person first, making things work for them and seeing happiness in their eyes that mattered more. Honestly, it takes a lot of pressure off you.

While I proudly claim I am great at multitasking (which

can also at times mean failing equally at a lot of things simultaneously), I used to be awful at concentrating fully on a single task. A compulsive daydreamer, my mind can easily drift away to the Malibu beach while stirring salt into my soup. But with the baby at home, I had to stay as alert as a Tai-Chi instructor. When I was holding him in one hand, trying to change his diaper, tipping his milk bottle with the other, avoiding getting peed on and preventing him from touching the electric wire in a groggy state at 2 a.m.—I couldn't afford to lose even one split second of alertness. There was a lot more at stake now, and I couldn't afford to be irresponsible with it.

A child is like your extensive and practical course in 'patience for dummies'. It starts right at pregnancy, when you feel life growing inside you bit by bit. You come to realize that things really happen when and how they have to, and there is not much you can do about them always. You have to hold those children for hours to make them sleep. You have to wait for them to finish their meals. You have to sit in your car, doing nothing, while they get their swimming lessons. You slog and slog the whole day, keeping your child happy, and by evening he smears his mouth with a marker you had hidden and hits you in the eye with his plastic bat. There were times when my son tested my patience so much that I found it hard to be the kind of mother I'd always imagined I'd be—calm, non-screaming, non-complaining, and one who would never use her iPad as a babysitter, even if for a few minutes a day. (Funnily enough though, while giving *you* the lessons on patience, those darned kids lose any ounce of patience they ever had in their systems to start with. Try switching channels for one single second when they are watching their cartoons and you will understand what I am talking about.)

It melts your heart to think how helpless those children are. Even if you do something wrong to them, they have no one apart from you to turn for solace. They want to grow up and become like you, so you better do a good job at being you, first, and then a sensible human that they can look up to.

I sometimes think I should have had this baby much earlier in life, for the new me has turned out to be far better than the old one. Yes, the new me has wrinkles on her forehead but they are from constant worrying about someone else. She has irreparable stretch marks on her stomach but each one of those marks reminds her of every breath, every yawn and every hiccup of her baby who once lived in there. She has dark circles under her eyes but they evoke those moments when her child woke up at nights to find comfort in her. She has flab that tells her that it is imperfections like these that make her life perfect.

Make way old me! The new me comes with a heart that is much bigger and much fuller than you could ever have!

His Majesty—the Invincible, the Unrestricted, the Toddler

Drums rolled. Bugles played. Flowers showered from the heavens above. The sky lit up with thousands of stars. Trees did a salsa. Dogs hopped on two paws. Pink elephants trumpeted in unison. Dolphins splashed water as they jumped in and out of the ocean. Parrots took circular flights with balloons tied to their tails. A monkey shot confetti in the air. Clouds burst to pour glitters by the kilos. Bells tinkled as dictated by a circus clown. A boat full of balls rowed through the stream and knocked at our door. Trains stopped in their tracks, to let the chicken cross who delivered the cake. Ducks carried little presents on their backs.

> *Moon is one*
> *So is the sun*
> *Who else is one?*
> *Our darling son!*

A year has gone
At crack of dawn
Shut eyes, big yawn
Our cutie was born
Cotton candy smell
Cheeks that swell
Twinkles a little jewel
Oh the joy none'd tell

Fingers all curled up
Lay like a pup
Daddy all night up
Watching over bub

Smiling in his sleep
Still counting sheep?
Legs like froggy leap
While birdies cheep

Want to see a chuckle?
Give that tummy tickle
Or fly him for a giggle
Leave him as he wiggles

Now he can walk
And some baby-talk
Time flew tick-tock
Wish'd kept days in lock

Unaware, he'd play
While we dance away

To revel this very day
And sing, happy birthday!

So after a lot of blood, sweat, tears, smiles, poetry and goo, we reached the one year mark.

'Congrats hon, we did it! As of tomorrow morning we will be officially trained in bringing up babies and keeping them intact for one year!' Hubby whispered in my ear as he emerged like a winner after putting our son to bed.

'I know, right! One full year, one lovely baby, countless fights, a million heartbeat skips and two happy parents who are still going strong!'

'Bro fist?'

'Yeah baby!'

'This marks as our first "parent birthday" too!'

'It does! So will you put him to sleep? I'm so excited for tomorrow; I don't think I will be able to sleep at all tonight!'

Of course the swirling parrots and other fantasy shebang above was not going to happen, but I was expecting the day to still somehow be different on his first birthday. Perhaps I was expecting a concrete milestone in my way with the Number 1 painted on it in black, or at least a finishing line pink ribbon with people waiting for me with Gatorade glasses and asking me to take a breather now. But I had to settle with a cake that my birthday boy threw up at night and about sixteen hundred failed attempts at making him sing happy birthday.

News flash: A one-year-old child is still a baby. Nothing dramatically changes in your life. He doesn't stop waking up in the nights and he does not become any less of work overnight. Or ever.

But this was a milestone nonetheless. This day marked for us the advent of yearly afternoons of sugar-high children bouncing off walls and eventually resulting in meltdowns—also known as 'birthday parties'. Now, I love those parties to be honest, just like I love everything that is crazy. My favourite ones are themed birthday parties that require weeks or even months of thinking, visualizing, collecting all associated craft supplies and finally buying everything readymade from an online shop. We did one around balls, since my son loved them and that was one of the total four words he could speak clearly by then. The other three being *mmmm, more* and *this*—all of which were abstract and hence did not qualify for a theme good enough to be displayed on Pinterest. The pressure we modern day parents live with these days!

So I got everything—a ball shaped fondant cake and round snacks and invitations, goodie bags, muffin toppers, banners, slingers and all other decoration around the same theme. I decorated our living room with actual balls and helium balloons that looked like balls, with Number 1 cut outs hanging from the roof and all other jazz. Husband, son and I wore similar shirts that said 'let's have a ball', with son's name printed on them. To all the neighbours in our apartment building, all of whom are senior citizens, we gave a big chocolate bar each that was shaped like the Number 1. It was our way to thank them for keeping up with our child's midnight clamour for the past one year and to bribe them for the years to come.

I was proud of myself for planning his birthday party like I would plan a project at work—complete with spreadsheets, to do lists and serious thinking for weeks. This was my attempt at exercising my brain that was almost dead by then. But as the parenting paradox would have it, the birthday boy slept through almost his entire party and was roped in once to cut the cake. His utterly visible annoyance at this forceful action of his parents was then duly captured in the camera for future memories before he was transferred back to his wonderland. Meanwhile, the other three kids that came among twenty adults, played with all his toys, sat on his swing and squealed at the paper whistles I blew.

I could have asked for my money back right there, if only that cake had not turned out to be heavenly.

For the first couple of years, kids are obviously not aware of the concept of birthdays or any other festivals. We are actually celebrating our own success there. My son always turned into the most unhospitable host whenever I invited people over. Watching big hands clinking glasses or big faces laughing out loudly when he was not even the centre of attraction was something he could never fathom. I think according to him the raison d'etre of the entire adult mankind was to serve him in one way or the other. 'So you are trying to say that there is life outside my world too?'

A few months after his birthday, it was Christmas. This time again I bought a massive tree and decorated it with all passion, hung out socks, wrapped presents and played carols on repeat in the living room for days. I was hoping to instill some Christmas-y spirit into my son. But he couldn't care any less. His letter to Santa would have read something like this:

Dear Santa,

Hope you haven't started from the North Pole yet. I am not exactly sure how Christmas works yet. My mom plans to dress me up in the kind of clothes you wear, because she thinks I am her very own personal you. Now that is a lot of pressure to be living with, if you ask me. Yes, I do believe that you are real and here Santa. Heck, I am only 15 months old and I even believe my mom when she points me to an imaginary airplane to make me stop crying. I understand that you deliver presents only to kids who have been good the whole year round. Now I don't have any concept of morals and virtues yet, so you can give me the benefit of doubt there. I did drive my parents crazy a few times this year, but overall, I have been a good kid, so that's sorted.

Anyway, here comes my list of things, in no particular order, that I want for Christmas. (I could have asked for world peace and all, but I can barely say peace without making it sound like fish, so let's drop the judging right there.)

- ☆ *An all-day, uninterrupted pass to a bathroom so I can flush the toilet as many times as I want and unroll and tear the toilet paper.*
- ☆ *My very personal vacuum cleaner—not a toy one,*

mind you. (You can use Mom's iPad to order it from Amazon, it's easy. I don't like to boast but I have reached as far as adding stuff to Mom's shopping basket on Amazon all by myself when she left it unattended.)

☆ *Easily reachable power sockets without any baby-proofing nonsense, installed in my room, low enough for me to reach and insert my fingers into.*

☆ *A couple of knives, paper cutters, scissors, screw drivers and anything else you have in that area. Match sticks will work like a charm, too.*

☆ *A recently and very neatly arranged wardrobe full of clothes. It should be easy enough for me to open and get into, so that I can throw all clothes on the floor. Even better if there is fragile stuff like crockery inside.*

☆ *Toiletries—shampoo, soap, oil, lotion, toothpaste—anything works really, as long as I am able to squeeze it into my mouth. Even dish-washing liquid or detergent will work equally well.*

☆ *Miscellaneous small metal or plastic objects that can pose a choking hazard. You can safely pick anything that says not suitable for kids under three.*

☆ *Tightly packed wet wipes, which when I take all out can never be stacked in the packet again.*

☆ *The itsy bitsy spider that climbed up the water spout. I have the rhyme, duh. I want the real spider. And…*

☆ *The book titled 'How to survive on little or no sleep*

for years. Now available with a free, lifelong supply of caffeine-powered energy boosting pills that will have you dancing to itsy bitsy spider's antics at 6 a.m. on weekends'—for Mom.

That should be it for now, Santa. I will be busy taking off and breaking all baubles that Mom aims to decorate the Christmas tree with. So I may not check the chimney every day, but I do hope I will get everything in time.

A very merry Christmas to you!
P.S. Ho Ho Ho to you too!

So yes, in theory, my son was now big enough to ask Santa what he wanted. In reality too, he was no longer a baby, but a full-fledged toddler now.

Question: What is a toddler?

Answer: A toddler is anthropomorphized noise, with dirt on his hands and stickers on his legs. He looks like a two feet jumping jack with a critical case of obsessive compulsive disorder. He talks in holophrases and his vocabulary is primarily dominated by the word 'No'. This is the first word he utters as soon as he wakes up and this is the word he ends his day with.

These are some scientific rules a toddler goes by:

Toddler don't-tell-me-what-to-do law of motion: *A toddler continues to be in his state of continuous activity unless he is acted upon by an external force.*
Example activity: Smudging the walls with sketch pens.

Example external force: A yelling mom, haplessly trying to snatch the damn pen out of his tiny clutches before googling ways to remove ink stains from the walls in a rented house.

(**Caveat:** The external force is almost never successful and often acts a tad too late. Also, buying your toddler sketch pens in the first place is one of the ways parents dig their own graves.)

Toddler in-your-face law of action reaction: *Every parental action force carried out for the benefit of the toddler is always opposed by an equal and opposite reaction force by the toddler.*

Example parental action force: Asking the toddler to put his books back on the shelf to enhance his stacking skills.

Example opposite reaction force: Toddler throwing all books on the floor and tearing off a few pages, emptying the laundry basket, hurling his toys across the room, pulling the curtains down with all his might—will all constitute to one unit of reaction force.

Toddler if-it-exists-I-will-break-it law of deconstruction: *If there is any way to do something wrong, the toddler most definitely will.*

Example something: Operating a device. Any device. That has a regular way of functioning and has some buttons on it.

Example wrong action: ( )itting on laptop ( )creen and ( ) mashing the key( ).

(The 'S' key on my laptop only works sometime, thanks to my boy. There, it ( )topped working again.)

Toddler if-it-exists-I-will-hide-it-and-forget-about-it law of spatial disorientation: *If anything is missing in the house just think of the last place you'd expect to find it.*
Example anything: My mobile phone.
Example the last place I'd expect to find it: The freezer. End of real story and the life of that phone.

Toddler three-pronged-sleep theory:
Toddler who sleeps early, wakes up early.
Toddler who sleeps late, wakes up early.
On a weekend, toddler wakes up earlier than usual.

Toddler love-in-the-time-of-flu concept of affection:
The number of hugs and kisses you get from your toddler is directly proportional to the amount of snot he is carrying in his nose at that time and inversely proportional to how badly you want those hugs and kisses from him.

Toddler barter economics principles for a fair trade:
If you want your toddler to give you your phone, give him your laptop. If you want to take the keys from him, give him your glasses to break. If you want to clean the kitchen, let him in the bathroom to create a mess there.

Toddler 'sound' sleep concept of irony:
A toddler will sleep through hours of drilling machines going on in the house but will wake up at the sound of you quietly putting your head down on the pillow. Empirically tested multiple times. The experiment has never failed.

Toddler laws of claimed ownership:
Everything in the world belongs to the toddler.

If something is in your hand, it is definitely his.
If something is in your plate, he wants to eat it.
If you give him something, he doesn't want it.

Toddler omnipresence principle of not letting adults do anything:
A toddler will always be in the way whenever an adult tries to do something that even borders on being important. Try to put your socks on to go out and toddler will run away with your one shoe. Try to cook his lunch and he will interfere with the stove knobs. Try to cut some vegetables and he will scarily try to interject his fingers into the act.

Toddler if-you-don't-repeat-you-retreat mantra of life:
Once a toddler learns to walk, he will walk all day. Once he learns how to talk, he will talk all day. It is not his problem if he doesn't make any sense. It is yours that you are unable to get into his mind and understand what he is saying—like why does he keep on repeating 'babysit bus', when he is already going somewhere in a car, for example.

Toddler get-away-with-murder-with-some-loving code of conduct:
For every 5 minutes of terrorizing their parents, toddlers grant you with a moment of pure love and cutest of the faces. It is a trap that you keep falling for over and over again, and toddlers know pretty well how to milk it.

A toddler's life is the only one worth living for. Toddlers are under no obligation to listen to you or to anyone else. They walk around and throw things like they rule the world, well at least yours they definitely do. They are just like vanity divas minus the money. They smear some paint incoherently on a drawing book and everyone exclaims like they are Picasso's reincarnation. Keeping them dirt free is your responsibility, not theirs. A single trip to a supermarket with my toddler running around and picking every jam bottle is enough to exhaust my self-embarrassment quota for one year. I have come to realize that half of parenting is about asking your child to do something and rest half is about dealing with the vehement refusal you get.

Reasoning with your toddler is like explaining to a drunken guy at a bar why he doesn't need that sixth drink. You can't even punish toddlers as they are too little for that, and they might even make a peekaboo game out of the timeout you give them in another room. But they are big enough to strategize how to climb up to the uppermost cupboard of the kitchen. (I do feel like giving myself a timeout, though—the idea of sitting quietly and being ignored for some time sounds utterly enchanting.)

A typical morning in my house started something like this:

'No.' (*Toddler wakes up and tells the world that he won't sleep any longer.*)

'Go back to sleep baby, it is still early.'

'No. Boot.' (*I want my book now.*)

'Okay, here you go.'

'Boooot.' (*Not my book, smarty pants. I want that little black one with light in it that you were reading last night.*)

'Here, take my Kindle but don't throw it on the floor.'

'Ta-tyu.' (*Thank you. I will first buy a book on it that you didn't want, and THEN throw it on the floor.*)

Bam!

'What did you do? I told you not to throw it; you are not getting it again.'

'Mama, Mama, Mama.'

<Faint cry>

<A little louder>

<A little louder>

<Slap!>

'Why are you hitting me baby? Okay, we are getting up. Wait, didn't you sleep late last night? Do you still not understand the concept of sleeping more to make up for late bedtime?'

<VERY LOUD CRY>

'Okay, getting your milk.'

8 seconds walking to the kitchen + 3 seconds of pouring milk in the bottle + 40 seconds of microwaving + 8 seconds walking back to the room = A toddler crying so loudly you think he might throw up—that too, over 200 ml of milk. I mean, raise your standard, kid.

3 minutes of rest while the toddler finishes his bottle. Mama is thinking if in that time she should go to the bathroom, have a sip of water, cover her freezing feet with socks or dare to put her head down on the pillow.

And time's up.

'Okay, let's change your diaper now.'

'No.'

'Lie down, baby.' *(While lifting Toddler's legs up with one hand and pushing his chest down with the other.)*

'No stop no stop no...' *(I don't want to lie down now, sleepy time is over. Stop pushing me down. Stop pulling my legs back. I have to run, you lazy woman. Stop stopping me. I am sliding down the bed. Why did you bring me back up, I am going to slide again. We can play this game the whole day, or you let me free. You won't listen? So off I go!)*

'Wait, don't run around naked, I still have to put your pants on. Where did you go? Damn! The bathroom door is open!'

Splash, splash, splash—one tiny hand goes in the pot and one picks up the toilet cleaning brush.

'Don't you dare put that hand in your mouth, you dirty, dirty boy. Wait, I should perhaps tell you to put it in your mouth, so you do the opposite. What kind of people forget to put child locks on the toilet seat!'

10 minutes, some wrestling and a lot of running later, pants are on the tiny bum.

Toddler: 0; Mommy: 1

So far so good.

Toddler has scooted to the kitchen now after switching the washing machine on and attempting to throw a dining chair on himself on the way. Mommy is headed to the bathroom.

'Bedd' *(I want to eat bread).* 'Maana' *(I want to eat banana too).*

'Bedd, bedd. Maana, maana. Bedd maana bedd maana

maana bed...' (*Keep repeating until you melt Mommy's brain, and the banana and bread come waltzing together and land into your hands.*)

'Wait, don't go to the kitchen, Mama is coming.' (*Desperate call from bathroom.*)

'Bedd bedd maana maana. Tadhaaaam!'

'What happened? Shucks the dishwasher was open.'

The pressure cooker is on the floor, along with some other pans. A tiny hand is just about to grasp a knife when Mommy runs to the kitchen for her life.

Kitchen damage abated. Phew, that was close!

Toddler: 0; Mommy: 2

Still going strong.

'Here's your bread. Sit peacefully on your high chair and eat.'

'Bedd.' (*I want bread in both my hands.*)

'Here, take another piece in the other hand, but you have to put your toy mop down then.'

'No.'

FRUSTRATED CRYING. (*Why do I have to let go of one thing to get another, this is totally impractical!*)

Mommy goes to the kitchen to make her cup of tea.

'Watta watta watta watta.' (*I want water, and I want it now, else I will dehydrate.*)

'Here's your cup, I am going to brush my teeth now.'

'Mama, Mama, Mama, aaah, ehhhh, aaaah.'

'Damn, did he just fall off the chair? Wait, that can't happen.'

'What do you want baby?' (*From a fluffy, toothpaste stuffed mouth.*)

'Poo, poo.'

'So you pooped? Let's change your diaper.'

'No.'

And loop back to the diaper-changing brawl that happened 15 minutes back. Kill me now, thinks Mommy.

'Leave your cup back at the table; you will spill water on your clothes.'

'No.' (*Do you want me to let you change my diaper? Then let me hold the cup.*)

'Ok, you are fine to go now. Wait, you spilled water on your pants!

Loop back to the ordeal of putting pants on someone who runs away. Kill me twice over, thinks Mommy.

Toddler: 1; Mommy: 2

And toddler is back in the game.

Disposing the diaper and washing hands peacefully.

Silence for 2 seconds, 3, 4, 5…10! Oh, Mommy could get used to this.

'How did you get into my wardrobe? Wait, don't throw my clothes on the floor. Not that dress, and that and that and not the socks for heaven's sake. Stop licking my shoes. Come out of the room. Don't open that drawer. Nooooooo!'

4 minutes later—Mount Fuji has erupted in the bedroom that was cleaned last evening and toddler appears

from underneath it, wearing all of Mama's underwear around his neck.

Toddler: 2; Mommy: 2

Even Steven.

🪀

'Going to take shower, you play outside.'

2 seconds after shutting the door.

Bam, bam, bam! *(Why did you abandon me outside, don't you love me?)*

And that's the end of Mommy's shower.

Toddler: 3; Mommy: 2

The game is getting interesting now.

🪀

'Ok, let me get ready now.'

Tiptoe, tiptoe, tiptoe—tiny feet sneak into the bathroom and come out with clothes and socks completely drenched.

'You've got to be kidding me. I have to change you again?'

Toddler: 4; Mommy: 2

🪀

'We are really, really late now. Want me to tell you who is mommy? Lie down quickly so I can change you.'

'No.'

'Please baby, I beg of you, let me change you.'

'No.'

'Okay, here—take my phone and throw it. Take this toothpaste and squeeze it. Here's my body lotion, lick it—do whatever you want, just stay still for a minute, will you?'

'No.'

'Okay, pull my hair then.'

Toddler: 5; Mommy: 2

Looks like an easy victory for the toddler now.

Clothes changed, yet again.

'Aa aa aa...*thish beddd.*' (*Little finger pointing at my toasted bread smeared with cheese.*)

'But you just had yours!'

'Waaa waaaa waaaaaaaaaaaaa.' (*I WANT YOUR BREAD, YOU SELFISH WOMAN.*)

'Ok, have it.'

Toddler: 6; Hungry Mommy: 2

'Let's walk to our car now.'

Toddler walks with Mommy to the car, planning his next move. Mommy is unlocking the car and putting her bag in. Toddler turns 180 degrees and scoots away.

'Stop, get back!'

Mommy runs again to bring the toddler back.

'No, Mama you stop! Baby help, Mama no help.' 'Eeeenough!' Toddler wants to get into the car and buckle up on his own.

'Okay do it.'

Toddler wastes Mommy's 20 minutes trying to do something he is not capable of but is too proud to let go.

Toddler: 7; Hungry-late-for-her-appointment Mommy: 2

🍼

'Wheels of the bus go round and round, round and round'—Mommy singing in the car to entertain toddler.

'No.'

'Old MacDonald had a farm ee...aai...ee...aai...o.'

'No, no, no. No song.'

No more singing in the car.

Toddler: 8; Hungry-late-for-her-appointment-dejected-not-even-allowed-to-sing Mommy: 2

And it was not even 9 a.m. yet. Welcome ladies and gentlemen to the world of terrible toddlerhood—what you saw just now was just the tip of the iceberg.

🍼

At around 18 months, I planned my first ever travel with my son. Before this he had not even been on a road trip that was longer than 30 minutes and here we were talking about a long haul international flight. I had been procrastinating this trip all this while. It was always too hot, too cold or too tiring to travel all the way to India with a baby. He still needed some vaccinations, you know. Let him be a little bigger so he can enjoy more. Perhaps, wait for him to be toilet trained. Or start eating more like adults. Or start filing his own taxes, maybe? But the family back home was getting antsy and I had to take him on his first ever flight—for eight hours, plus another seven to wait for a connecting domestic flight and an hour more on that flight—which when all added up felt like more than a lifetime.

At the end of it all my hair had turned grey and I was looking for a baby-proofed box to store my dentures in.

I was going to travel all by myself and Hubby was going to join us later as he couldn't get enough holidays from work. We mulled over it a lot, but couldn't figure out a way to travel together. The more I thought about it, the more I dreaded it. So I decided to rip the Band-Aid off in one go and just go ahead and take that flight. I made three separate checklists of things to pack—one for the cabin, one for check-in and one for anything else I could stuff in my jacket pocket that was needed immediately. The lists were very exhaustive, like the one for cabin had 'food' on it for example. Talk about having organizational skills.

Now the internet is abundant with tips to travel with your toddler, telling you how to make the flight easy for both you and your child. I sifted through a lot of information around that, just so I could be ready for any challenges that could come my way. But when it actually came to flying with my toddler, none of that came to my rescue—just like that hypnobirthing book or various other parenting books I had devoured as if I was preparing for a civil services exam.

For instance, there was one suggestion about giving a pacifier or a lollipop to your toddler to suck on when the flight took off, so his ears won't hurt. But what they didn't tell me was how I could keep that lollipop safe from the toddler's hands when he tried to test gravitational laws by hurling it far away in the aircraft while you were busy buckling his seat belt. Nowhere did I find any mention of ways on how to deal with the situation when you have cleared security check, are waiting to board and your toddler poops inside that cordoned area where the only bathroom around has no changing table for babies.

But now that I had been there, done that and sworn to not repeat it anytime soon, I came up with my own set of very practical tips that can definitely help anyone planning to fly with their toddler. The tips don't involve any lollipops.

Tip 1: Don't travel with your toddler. No seriously, just try to explore this option and save yourself from reading the rest of this list. I mean, nothing will really change in the world if you didn't travel. If you have waited so long, just wait a little while longer, preferably until you can threaten him into believing that the aircraft will explode if he asked for another glass of juice. Mine didn't understand that simple logic and just wailed, but I hope that in a few years he will.

Tip 2: Book a separate seat for your toddler, even if he is less than two years old. That seat will come in handy to keep all that stuff your toddler wants and then doesn't want the next minute and wants again. If you are lucky, he may even like to sit on that seat for a few minutes and watch the in-flight TV, which he will insist on operating with the remote of your seat. So don't pin your hopes on watching the latest movie during your flight.

Tip 3: Pack like your plane is going to land on Jupiter. I had even packed soap bubble making kits in my handbag to use on the aircraft if nothing else worked in entertaining my son. (Not sure if the gravity levels at Jupiter would have allowed me to blow the bubbles, though.)

Now would be your chance to go back to Tip 1.

Still no?

Tip 4: Your toddler will want to walk through the aircraft to the emergency door, to the crew area or to the lavatories—90 per cent of the time that he is awake. So hold a placard that all passengers can clearly read, which says:

> *I know he is cute, but I don't know what YOU did with your hands right before now. So don't touch him.*
>
> *P.S.: Do I know you, for you to offer us the contact of your skin? I don't care if he reminds you of the son you never had.*

Yelling at someone AFTER they have already touched your baby will serve no purpose. I learnt it the hard way.

Tip 5: Do something to constipate your toddler for the flight if you can. A day or a half without poop never hurt anyone. The obnoxiously loud and rat hole sized toilets in the flight will scare the living daylights out of your toddler and shoot up your anxiety levels. If it is just a regular diaper change, do that on the seat itself when flight attendants are not looking. (Don't judge me there. Just because I am a mom, doesn't mean that I care for the world around me.)

Tip 6: On the airport, don't introduce your toddler to fancy stuff like moving walkways or vending machines, if you plan to board the flight on time. It won't matter what time of the day you decide to fly, the wide running spaces and brightly lit airports will always guarantee that your toddler is as wide awake as an owl. In the 20 plus hours it took us to reach, my son had slept for barely an hour and a half and was running on massive amounts of adrenaline through airport corridors at 3 a.m.

Tip 7: A mom with a small child will always get priority. Shamelessly ask for it, ignoring the rolled up eyes of other non-parent passengers. Remember that they were children themselves at some point. Remind them if need be—you will feel great about yourself for having done that. As moms we handle enough literal crap every day to not be willing to take anyone else's figurative crap anymore.

Tip 8: Don't expect to watch TV, read, eat, sit, stretch, sleep, drink or pee in peace. Treat the flight as a regular day at home with your toddler—with extra crankiness, boredom, limited mobility and sleep-time distractions added to the mix. Good luck!

Tip 9: Don't imagine that all will be well once you land at your holiday destination. There is no holiday for a mom. The toddler will still wake up early, need food, snacks, baths and diaper changes. The earlier you burst your pre-baby holiday concept bubble, the better it will be for your sanity.

It was obviously a much awaited event for both my husband and my families in India to have our son visit them for the first time. He loved the attention he got there. And it was funny to see them all baby-talk with him in their own ways. I mean, I even think in baby language all the time, but hearing someone else do it just sounds very otherworldly for some reason. The family went a bit overboard in their excitement too to ensure they handled the NRI baby well. Even his bath water was filtered and then warmed up. His room was pest controlled every couple of hours—one person was armed with the tennis racquet thingy and given the direction to kill any mosquito on spot. The doors were kept sealed when he slept lest he should get disturbed by the sounds of vegetable vendors. He was free to pee anywhere in the house. He was given the otherwise prohibited sugary juices and cookies whenever he wanted by the grandparents. It was like a trip down to Willy Wonka's chocolate factory for him. A huge religious ceremony was organized in his honour with friends and relatives invited from everywhere—even though he slept though most of it. And soon enough it was time for us to go back, which brought me to the next tip for flying with toddlers:

Tip 10: Breathe in, breathe out. This too shall pass. And in no time will you be boarding your return flight (which will be equally long and tiring as the onward one, just so you remember). The toddler will have a ball during the trip—so that's your only saving grace in this entire ordeal. You will get your money, time and sanity's worth by just watching him shriek in excitement to be in the *aerrroooplane*.

Happy flying!

It's Still Not the End. Neither Do I Want It to Be

Time is a shy little thing. If you keep looking at it, waiting for it to move, it just won't budge. But if you turn your back to it and start doing something else, it will fly. Just like that little child who drills a hole in your brain the whole day by singing his favourite rhyme over and over again, but goes mum when asked to sing it in front of your twenty house guests intently looking at him. (That this overzealous display of your child's skills in front of other uninterested outsiders should be banned by law, is a topic for another discussion, however.)

Before I became a mom, time did not have a great importance for me. I mean, of course I had to reach work at a certain time, wake up at a certain time, and catch a show on TV at a certain time. But it sort of always ran in the background, at a pace I had unconsciously adjusted to and was fine with. I never waited for it to move quicker or wanted for it to stop where it was.

But after my son's birth, time found a new meaning in my life, and I started to be affected by it more than ever before. Sometimes time moves way too sluggishly for me when I am waiting for the cleaner to come in just so my son has something else to entertain him with, as I am running out of games to play with him that last for longer than a minute. Other times it goes by a zip-zap speed when I see one evening that his clothes don't fit him anymore, the ones that I had bought only a month ago.

Today, when I look back at his pictures or videos, I find it hard to believe that this two-year-old is the same clueless infant who once cooed from his crib and was attached to my body the whole day long. And now he can walk up the steps, holding dearly to a railing, slowly putting one foot ahead, joining it with the other and squealing at his arrival. He can scoop a spoon, toss out a fallen blueberry when he doesn't want it, tell me when he wants more, and roll his sleeves up when it is time to wash hands. He knows that when you go out you wear a *daddit* (jacket) and when you come back you take your *shush* (shoes) off, and he is almost always talking or running or doing both his entire awake time.

Just yesterday he had learnt to crawl on all fours through my feet and the dining table, to eat with his hand and pick at what I ate, staring at me like a soft little pup, to slide down the couch carefully, legs first. Just yesterday he had learnt to sit, clap and sway to music, roll over to reach his rattle and stick his tongue out at the first taste of pulpy carrots. Just yesterday he had exited my body and landed into my arms, turning his head when I snapped my fingers.

It really does feel like yesterday now.

Childhood is indeed fleeting. Strangely enough, things happen so slowly and yet so quickly at the same time. The adult life is so stagnant. Scrolling through your Facebook page in 10 minutes, you can come across birthday wishes for three consecutive years and nothing would have dramatically changed. We go through changes like increasing and decreasing waistlines, moving countries and jobs, reading new books and making new friends. But the change we see going through our children dwarfs any of that.

Right in front of our eyes they move diaper sizes up and their tub baths give way to showers. They suddenly stop waking up for a milk bottle in the night and start repeating the swear words we accidentally utter in front of them. There is always something new to look forward to with them each day. Parenting forces us, in a good way, to stop every now and then to smell the lilies. A baby reminds us to look at that brilliant show called 'life' that nature has put up around us, anytime without ticket from the back seat—which we otherwise miss in our daily rigmarole.

Sometimes when I sat playing with my son, and was too tired to stack his plastic rings and take them all out for the twenty-sixth time, I'd take the phone out of my pocket and sneakily check my email or message my friends when he wasn't looking. One evening when I had left the phone to charge, I sat with him as he played with one of his similar, repetitive toys. Every now and then I would show interest in his play. While I got lost in some thought, looking out of the window for some time, he came up to me with little concerned eyes and said, 'Mama, phone?'

It broke my heart. My son had sensed that Mama was bored and hence she should get the phone to entertain her or do something more important. I had an immediate epiphany at that point. I thought that by distracting myself away from my son's vanilla world that was so beautifully devoid of any action, I could be letting precious moments slide through my fingers. And yet, I was lamenting that time was flying.

I realized that I should not look *away*, but look *at* him when he was growing up. I shouldn't hurry him up but stay with him to pluck those leaves when he wants to. I shouldn't clean the house when he asks me to play ball with him. I shouldn't take him to the car if he wants to run after that chirping birdie. I shouldn't get angry when he laughs at the moonbeam at 2 a.m.

It is totally possible that I was reading too much in between the lines of a half sentence spoken by a baby who could barely talk then. He may not have implied anything of what I interpreted. He could have been asking for the phone to play with *Talking Tom* on it after all. But either way, it was enough to interrupt my pointless thinking and bring me back to where I had mentally drifted from.

'No, Mama doesn't need her phone,' I replied, as I gave my son a kiss on his cheek.

My son started going to a daycare a few days in a week now and he likes it there. I thought it would be good for him to go out into the world and socialize a bit. This time I was under no pressure to make the daycare work for him unlike last time, since I was still at home. He likes to explore new places and gain new experiences. He comes home and imitates other children there and we have a big laugh—it's the first ever secret between the two of us. With him happily settled there, I started working on those days too, and will soon be back to working full-time. Although, there are days when I still feel guilty of inflicting this separation on him. I often expected a dramatic reunion with my son when I went to pick him up at the daycare—similar to the ones arranged by the Salvation Army—full of hugs and tears. Not only has nothing of that sort ever happened, but also my son is always found having so much fun with his little friends that he doesn't want to go home with me, at least not that soon—much to my embarrassment, mixed with some dollops of envy. The parenting joke is always on you, never on the child.

The oft heard cliché of parenting is, 'You don't even get to know when your kids grow up.' During the first few months of my son's life, I never agreed to that. You so know when you are nursing him like a clockwork, you so know when he is waking up every hour in the night, you so know when he is acting up, you so know when he gets his first shots and cries helplessly. Outsiders don't, but parents for sure get to know and feel the struggle of bringing up a child every single day. There were days when I wanted it all to pass and waited for my son to quickly grow up.

But here I am now after two years. Squeezing some seconds from that meeting. Running to catch that 3 minute earlier metro. Praying that I get all green signals on the way to reach to him quickly. Waiting for him to wake up once before I go to sleep. *Shishing* (sitting) with him to build his castle of blocks immediately when we get home with my boots still on and bladder almost bursting. Somehow hoping that all that time I collect will add up to be enough to redeem his past.

But it is never enough.

The lazy afternoons when I am home and playing *row, row, row your boat* on the piano for him, I wish I could press pause on time. I have grown to become more insecure of time now, trying in vain to capture it. But it always outruns me, asking me to live the moments rather than chase them.

A friend, married for five years now, told me he doesn't see the need to have children. And so doesn't his wife who is past thirty and hence is being advised by everyone and their nosy aunts to watch her biological clock. Pestered by others showing curiosity into his procreating plans all the time, he turned to me and asked, 'Can you give me three good reasons to have children?'

I honestly could not think of even one that could satisfy him and replied with, 'Well, my child is the best thing that has ever happened to me. I can't imagine my life without him.'

'But that is something you say now,' pat came his repartee, 'you didn't know of this beforehand, so why *did* you take the plunge?'

I just shrugged off with, 'Oh, I don't know, I just felt like. I loved kids anyway,' and moved on to steam carrots and peas for my son's dinner. ('More *tarrots* and *peesh*, Mama'—he'd demanded.)

When I was being fielded with, 'When are you having a baby?' questions, I had a strong urge to reply with—'Why don't *you* tell me what works for you according to your busy schedule? I will time my pregnancy around that.' Those questions are not just rude in a mind-your-own-damn-business sort of way, but they can also be extremely hurtful to someone who has been longing to have a baby and for some reason is unable to. Then there are some who just don't want to have kids—not now, not later.

And I totally agree with them when they say that there shouldn't be a reason to not have kids.

Just like I feel there shouldn't be a reason to have kids, either. At least not a logically analysed one. Which is probably why I went blank when asked to cite not one but three of those supporting my decision. Here's the thing about our society. We are wired to think of everything that we do as a means to an end. We want to buy a TV, because we want some entertainment at home. We want to go on a holiday, because we are bored of our routine. We cultivate a hobby, so we can ultimately turn it into a passion and if possible, into a profession. There is always anticipation for a better life behind every action we take. But when we run the baby question through this logic, we don't get an answer. Since a baby is something unseen and unheard of, you never know what it will do to your life and you can almost never return it to the store like that TV, if you didn't like it.

Parenting is the exact opposite of all that kind of rational thinking. I have come to realize that if there is one situation in life where we are forced to just flow with nature—it is parenting. Parenting is about plans falling in their face and you having to play by the day. It is about letting go, jumping in and trusting your instinct to get you through. How often do we do that in our otherwise, overly-calculated life?

Some say that mothers can never have it 'all'—clean houses, happy children and fat paychecks all together. I would say that the 'all' here is very relative and there is no one formula to define it for everyone. We sometimes think that a baby's arrival will disrupt the equilibrium that we have in our lives. But what we don't realize is, that the equilibrium is built of mouldable clay and not concrete. It can easily be flattened out. A baby only adds another shade of clay in there, which when all mixed up with our original dough, becomes homogenous and can again be moulded into a new, mostly better and more colourful equilibrium.

I used to think working in a stressful job was tough and then I had a baby. I thought being a stay-at-home mother full-time was tough—requiring you to speak in monologues, not exercing your brain the way you do at work and feel unaccomplished despite having toiled the whole day long. And now I think being a working mother and balancing it all out is tough. Getting the child ready to leave in the morning to reach work on time when he doesn't want the breakfast you have made, will eat only in the orange butterfly plate that is lying dirty in the sink and will leave the house only if you find his small fire engine that he forgot after hiding somewhere—are the kind of predicaments that can tire you out even before your day has started. Juggling drop-off and pick-up responsibilities with your spouse, managing work deadlines and their associated stress, bringing everything to a standstill when he is not keeping well, spending enough quality time with your child while keeping guilt at bay, taking care of yourself and your house, having fun with friends, keeping up with your hobbies—I have realized that the only way I can live happily is by not really wanting to have the 'all' as defined by the society around me. That blissful moment when you pick up your child after a tiring day at work with a beaming smile and a million stories from him on how his day went, is all you need to keep it going. (Together with some Red Bull.)

In the rare case that you haven't inferred from this book, hidden under those harried experiences, I have talked enough about how positively motherhood has transformed my life. Or about how, before my baby I never knew it would be possible to love someone this much. Or about how I have slept with a smile on my face every night since he was born (after he slept, that is).

But I didn't do any of that with an intention to create a case for parenting here. It is not about judging how much I invested and how much I have gained in this exercise. It is not about saying that it was all worth it in the end—because there is no end that I am seeking.

For the first time in my life I am actually seizing the moment, without keeping an eye on the future. For the first time I am scooping out as much life as I can from time, and to my surprise, life never seems to run out. For the first time it really is about enjoying the journey.

Just looking at my son (if I can resist kissing him) or

even thinking about him fills my body with a sort of positive energy that I never experienced earlier. It is like being in a lifelong meditation or trance, or, at the very least, that dream where you are just running and running happily and aimlessly in a wide open field without any end in sight. And it feels wonderful! My days as a mother include chasing birds, spotting airplanes, dancing to any music and building sand castles.

I can never put any of that into some kind of tangible logic and build a cause–effect, risk–reward framework around it. And that is perhaps why it is the most beautiful thing in the world.

Do you need a 'reason' to be happy? If not, then you don't need a reason to have kids too.

You may, unfortunately, need one to *stop* having them after one point, however.

One afternoon when I picked my son from the daycare, I decided to drive straight to the grocery store. He loves running errands with us, so whenever we can, Hubby and I make it a point to take him along to infuse some excitement into this drabbest of the chores.

But this one wasn't going to be a regular visit.

So I parked the car, took the stroller out from the boot and made my son sit in it. I then wheeled the stroller inside the store. All I had to pick was a loaf of bread and two watermelons. This could easily fit in the basket under his stroller so I did not carry any bags with me and didn't take one from the shop either. When we were done shopping, I did the normal routine of letting my son scan the things and giving him the receipt to feel important with. I folded the stroller and put it back in the boot and plonked my son on his car seat at the back, which after some struggle he agreed to comply with. I then put all the watermelons and bread on the front seat next to me and drove home.

Before we could reach home, my son started asking for the bread we had bought. I didn't want to give it to him, since it would have killed his appetite for the food I had cooked for him at home. But he attacked me in my most vulnerable state when I was still driving, so I had to give in.

Hang in there, the story doesn't end here.

So, I stopped the car near our house and took Sonny Boy out of his car's seat and made him stand. I then did something I shouldn't have done.

I opened the front seat door to take the watermelons, remainder of the bread, car keys and phone out. My clothes didn't have any pockets, and I wasn't carrying my handbag with me. While I was still bent over the seat, strategizing on how I could possibly pick all of that with but two hands, my son crept from my side and climbed up the front seat. It was a hallelujah moment for him to have access to the steering wheel, gear and buttons that made the wipers go *swish, swish, swish*. And so he set up shop there. Now he wouldn't come out, no matter how much I asked, pleaded, threatened, advised or bribed him. This went on for some time when I decided it was time for me to take charge.

'Okay baby, you stay here. Mama is going,' I thought I could fool him with this empty threat and make him come with me.

'Bye Mama,' he gave it back to me in my face, complete with a hand wave.

'I am closing the door now and leaving you inside,' I half-closed the car door and gestured at him from the window.

'Bye Mama,' he was least bothered.

CLICK!

Somehow the door got shut and the car got locked from inside—which can happen with our car, as I came to know later.

About two seconds later I realized, I HAD LEFT THE CAR KEYS INSIDE THE CAR!

My son was now inside a locked car, all on his own on a hot summer day with all windows rolled up.

I panicked my heart out. There was no one around me. I pulled the car door handles vigorously but they didn't give away. I knocked on the car windows to my son, but he just looked at me and continued to play with the steering wheel. I frantically searched for my phone to call Husband who was at work.

But my phone was inside the car too. I had no idea what to do then. I just stood there looking helplessly at my son who was trapped inside.

A few seconds later, I thought of signalling to him to press the unlock button from inside.

'Press that button baby. NOT THIS. THAT ONE,' I shouted over and over again as I pointed to it with my fingers. But he couldn't understand me and was distracted by all that was available at the driver's seat for him to play with. He pressed everything that was there, except that one button.

A few minutes later a woman parked her car next to mine. I rushed to her to borrow her phone and tried calling my husband. It took me a few tries to dial his number correctly, which under anxiety I had a hard time recalling. But he didn't answer. Meanwhile, I tried opening the car with the other woman's car keys in vain. She tried to call the car service people for me, but nobody answered there too.

I knocked at the car windows again and asked my son to pick up the car keys from the seat and try to unlock. But the car keys were no longer at the seat where I had left them.

He had taken them and inserted into the ignition as he had seen me doing that many times.

'Take the keys out!' I screamed.

He gave me a clueless look.

'Keys OUT. Keys OUT,' I kept shouting and gesturing.

'*Shtut* (stuck),' he replied.

'Try again. Keys out.'

'*Shtut* Mama.'

'Pull it out with both hands. BOTH HANDS. LIKE THIS. TWO HANDS. ONE TWO. ONE TWO.'

My brain froze and I couldn't think clearly under panic. While I was considering breaking the car window with a brick, my son somehow managed to get the keys out.

'PRESS THAT BUTTON ON THE KEY. PRESS PRESS PRESS!'

CLICK!

The car got unlocked.

Phew! I immediately opened the door and snatched the keys from him.

Now my son had obviously not realized the seriousness of the situation and was still unhappy at the prospect of being taken out of the car. He didn't want to let go of this accidental lottery that he had been indulging in for the last 20 minutes or so.

'A moment back you were asking me to operate those buttons in the car, now you want to take me away? No way am I coming out of here,' was what he meant to say to me.

So I had to pick him up forcibly; somehow unclenching the handbrake and gears from his hands and literally drag him out amidst his persistent, rebellious cries. The moment I got him out and made him stand, a watermelon rolled over and reached the ground a bit further away from the car. I laughed over it in order to present that as a joke to my son who was crying desperately like someone who was being kidnapped. The joke didn't work of course and he continued with his song of whine. I picked the car keys, house keys and phone in one hand, one watermelon in the other and bread on my arm folded against my body. I then bent down and picked the other watermelon from the floor.

Still with me?

Seeing me helpless, with no free hands to close and lock the car door with, my son started to make a dash towards the front seat again. So I rushed back to pull him out one more time with all my might and full hands. This time he protested much harder and cried even louder, but I somehow managed to pull him out again. The watermelon that had fallen down had cracked and its juice was all over me, my son's head and the car's seat by now. If I didn't clean the seat immediately, the stain would stay there. So I tried to now get to the tissue box in the dashboard, while balancing two watermelons and a loaf of bread, and blocking the open car with my torso moving from side to side to not let my son in for the third time. Since it was getting too much to handle, I placed the watermelons again on the seat and started to wipe the stains. Seeing all that drama, the other watermelon got excited and decided to take a plunge. It rolled over even farther on the ground, puncturing itself even worse than its brother.

My son on the side had gone stark raving mad by now. Before I could wipe the seat, I had to turn over to him to cool him down. But he wouldn't have any of my prodding and sat down like dead weight right there on the floor next to the car. He wouldn't budge now, no matter what I did or said. I decided to focus my energies on the other watermelon and unite it with its kin, and give my son some time to settle on his own. But he turned worse. So now I stood there in the middle of two wounded watermelons with their blood spilled all over me and the beautiful beige seat of my car, a screaming child and a wish for the earth to tear apart and swallow me.

Just then, an elderly woman walking her dog appeared on the scene. Looking at my plight, she stopped right where she was but gave me what I thought was a snarky smile. I smiled back apologetically at her, pretending that everything was all right.

'I can take care of this,' I said to myself before I went over to try and change grumpy grumpersome's emotional climate.

'Should we go home now baby?'
'No.'
'Do you want to talk to Papa on phone?'
'No, no, no.'
'Do you want to help me pick a watermelon?'
'Ye…noooooo. *Keeesh.*'
'Oh, you want keys. Here you go.'
'No, no, no.'

The old woman stood there and kept watching and smiling at us.

My son was hell bent on embarrassing me more by refusing to get off the ground. I took out the packet of bread and offered him. Perhaps it was my subconscious attempt to prove to that elderly lady that I was *really* trying my best there.

'Do you want more bread? See it's so nice!'

Of course he didn't want any bread now and he flung away, even the one that he had in his hand earlier. It was hot and I was sweating profusely after having dealt with our situation for the past 45 minutes and over. I was now that mother who had got her son locked out in a car, was unable to manage his tantrums in the middle of the road and one who couldn't hold her life or watermelons together.

I was almost in tears and I screamed in my head, 'DEAR GOD, WHAT HAVE I DONE TO DESERVE THIS? WHY IS THIS SO DAMN HARD?' Then I took a deep breath, locked the car, picked the house keys and phone, plopped the toddler on my hip, kicked those watermelons away and ran until I reached home. I'd had enough by then.

I went inside the elevator and pressed vigorously on the close button. No, I didn't have any patience left in me to have my son press it. I just wanted to get to my house and lock it from inside and not having to deal with my son running out again. I threw the keys and phone somewhere, put my son down and headed straight to the kitchen for a drink. Since it was only 5 p.m., I settled for an iced coffee. My son immediately switched his grouchy channel off and got busy with his business of throwing things around.

'Mama, come tent,' he hid inside his tent and invited me over for a game of hide-and-seek, like nothing had happened at all. But I stood in the kitchen still reeling from everything.

When sugar and caffeine started to act on my brain, I calmed down. I could have managed this better, I thought. I could have let my son play for a while in the car until he got bored with it. I could have been more careful and avoided him getting locked out. I could have carried a bag with me to store the watermelons. I could have left all the stuff inside the car to pick it later and could have just focused on my son. I could have not gone to the shop at all with him. It wasn't like I had gone to buy some lifesaving insulin for me. It was just a bloody watermelon for god's sake! I could have easily lived without it for another day. I could have totally ignored that old lady with the dog and her smile. I am not even sure if she was smiling *with* me to reassure me or smiling *at* me with derision.

I could have done a lot of things better, but I didn't. The moment had gone now and I had to move on too.

'Mama, *wai aaa you* (where are you)?' my son called for

me from the tent.

I peeped inside his tent and saw that everything in there was back to fun, happiness and living in the moment.

'Mama is here!' I said animatedly and rushed inside to pick him up in my arms. He gave me the world's biggest hug back.

I then took him to our balcony window and showed him a birdie walking on the ground. The birdie then disappeared behind a bush, next to which lay those watermelons, forlorn and in a dilapidated state.

A bit worried to not see his feathered friend anymore, my son called out to her, 'Birdie, *wai aaa you?*'

The moment I heard that, I burst out laughing.

'What did you just say?'

'Birdie, *wai aaa you?*'

'You are calling the birdie?'

'Yeah. Birdie *peesh tumm* (please come).'

I laughed even more. I laughed at his overwhelming cuteness. I laughed at those darned watermelons. I laughed at myself.

'Haha *ish* funny, Mama,' my son joined in the hysteria too.

I laughed and laughed till tears came rolling down my cheeks. And I fell in love with myself and my son all over again.

An Apologia to My Son

Dear Son,

When I was writing this book, I forgot that you will grow up one day and be able to read this on your own. And hence, I took the liberty to lay your baby-life bare here. But considering that even your body has been laid bare in front of people you don't even know, I hope you won't mind.

You see I am not good at clicking pictures and even worse at doing something with them. If I lose my phone one day, I would have lost all the moments of your babyhood that I might have captured in that. I know I need to keep a backup of those photos somewhere. But I can't be bothered with doing all that boring 'being organized' stuff when you have more interesting stuff to offer me with your cute capers. So I decided to pack all our memories in this book. When I will be old enough to not remember what I had for breakfast in the morning, you can read this book to me to remind me of our first years of knowing each other. I think by then you would have also realized that there is hardly any fun in tearing pages from a book, so I did not baby-proof this one.

I know I have made a lot of mistakes as a parent and I am still making them. But I hope you can forgive me.

I should also confess here that I have lied to you at more than one occasion:

- ☆ *When I told you we didn't have more M&Ms left in our house, I did that only to avoid giving a lot of sugar to you. Right after that I went back to the kitchen and stuffed my mouth with a handful.*
- ☆ *When you asked me for ketchup to mix in your yogurt, I acted as if I didn't understand what you were saying and distracted you by making silly faces.*
- ☆ *When you wanted to play with the vacuum cleaner that was locked in a closet, I pretended that I couldn't open it even when I always had the keys with me.*
- ☆ *I have told you many times that whatever is not available for you to see at any point is sleeping in its house. Like a public bus or a row-row boat. They are things son, they don't sleep.*

…and many more times like that. I may have to continue with my lying for a few more years until I can't trick you anymore. But I hope you will forgive me for that too.

If there is anything in this book that you don't agree with, let's settle that over a cup of chocolate milk. All right, I will let you have the whipped cream too.

I can't thank you enough for coming to my life. I don't know what I would have done without you. Thanks for giving me all those moments to write about. Thanks also for...

What the dirty diaper! You are up from your nap already?

Noooooooooo, don't play with my keyboa...

Slkhfiosyf90weuyfpwfhsjfs[of]-ofsof'sfo] apa0f0fw0owfowofw]ow==wfk;skfwif0-wf0686------wue wpofuwf7777777777lsjfdsshfdsfpsfshjf,,,,,,,,,,,,,,,,,,,,,,,slkdn gweopih23452355fewgtr34666^^^^^^^^^^ekuryt98 eqytef8g10057777ii3griugrof kalfz?v v]e m

Eihgio4hgiohgioehgioehgiqh3-9486—u-hg-ghpogepghejh39-rog[qqqgjejgegkeej

Fwlkehh39889493kgkgww=

Questions to Discuss with Other Parents

☆ How many times did the author make a booboo in this book?

☆ If booboo were a tangible object, what would it sound and look like?

☆ If the intent of the book was to not teach parenting, what exactly was it supposed to do?

☆ Is the author a bad mom?*

☆ Is the author the most wonderful mom ever?**

☆ Is it fair for the baby to think that his dad is cooler than his mom?

☆ What is the best way for the author to spend a Friday evening?

---

*I am watching you here and will hunt you down if you answer in affirmative.
**Bonus points for answering this one with… (You know what I mean.)

Appendix:
The New Mommy Alphabet

A is for Anxiety. Anxious Mom tiptoeing in the room like a thief to not wake up the baby. Over-anxious Mom biting her nails while peeing, thinking the baby would jump off the crib or such.

B is for Books. The fat parenting bibles that will tell you what babies should do and when. 'Honey, I think the baby is choking.' 'Wait, let me check in the book first if we are supposed to pick him up immediately or will doing that spoil him in the long run.'*

C is for Crying. Of babies when they need something or when they just want to test their own sound. And of their psychic moms from the guilt of being away from them or from watching them grow up every day.

D is for Diapers. Gazillions of them in the bins or strewn

---

*That never happened with us, by the way.

on the floor at night. They magically get dirty right after you have changed them. I once had a dream that the world was ending so I needed to stock up on diapers.

E is for Ex-husband, Ex-friends, Ex-peace, Ex-sleep, Ex-everything, Ex-your life. Oh the husband is technically there, but he calls you mommy now and you call him daddy.

F is for Forums, where you seek help from other frazzled parents.

G is for Dr Google. The biggest parenting adviser of our times.

H is for Hurry up, we are getting late. For our playgroup, for our swimming class, for our reading session, for our baby gym class. And for our bedtime—as we need to be fresh in the morning for all those classes.

I is for Illness. Babies get ill like crazy. And no one but a parent alone can think that their germy baby with a runny nose is still kissable.

J is for Job. The eternal question of whether you should join your job back after having a baby. The perpetual debate of—which job is more demanding? Hubby's office one or your stay-at-home one—the verdict of which will decide who gets to do laundry on the weekend.

K is for Keep calm and carry the heck on, Mama. No, seriously. Breathe in, breathe out, the baby will sleep only when he has to.

L is for Late to reach everywhere. Since you are never able to H for Hurry up after all, what with diaper emergencies right when you are about to leave or a general tantrum thrown in to add to the thrill.

M is for Milestone. By so and so age baby should be able to connect a pen drive into a USB port.

N is for No. No, you don't pull someone's hair when they come to hug you. No, you don't ask your mommy to flash her belly button in public.

O is for Others, who absolutely, one hundred per cent, stop bothering you once you have a baby. You have a whole new battle to fight and have no time for anyone or anything insignificant.

P is for Picking things from the floor. ALL. DAY. LONG. Eventually the floor becomes your place for storing things after you have put them back in their place for the 127th time.

Q is for Questions. Initially parents ask all the questions and also answer them. 'Do you want to have that tasteless mashed broccoli? Yes, you do!' Later on, question asking becomes the turf of children, while parents have to succumb to a 'because I said so' after having exhausted all sane replies to the incessant stream of their whys.

R is for Repetition. You are not a parent until you haven't sung your child's favourite song at least 256 times a day, and displayed excitement at each run.

S is for Sleep, or the lack of it. Enough said.

T is for Themed birthday parties. Once upon a time this world was a very happy place. People celebrated birthdays, ate cakes, gave presents and slept back at home peacefully. Then came Facebook and Pinterest. And the advent of themed birthday parties.

U is for Unused toys and other baby contraptions. We need to stop tricking those children with pretend toys. The real stuff at home does the job better.

V is for Very happy. Despite all the hard work they require, those babies always make their parents happy, very happy.

W is for Weight. And the obsession to reach a certain number by a certain birthday. And the longing look at those pre-pregnancy denims hanging at a wardrobe corner. And the mellow sigh to see them not fit anymore. And the revengeful determination to workout. And the clandestine giving in to a helping of cake. 'Darn it, I need those calories to be able to look after the baby.'

X is for Xylophone, as it says in the alphabet books that you remember by heart now.

Y is for You. It only seems apt that this comes at the end of the alphabet. Since parenting is a game that children own. So, them and their things first.

Z is for Zzzzzzz. I need to doze off now. Remember to sleep when the baby sleeps as all the B for Books say.

Acknowledgements

I would like to thank from the bottom of my heart and in no particular order:

☆ My husband for suggesting the title of this book, and for all other similar acts that require the least effort but still are indispensable in the greater scheme of things—bringing our baby into this world for instance. And for being the best dad and the best husband ever. (You have been winning those two by default for many years now.)

☆ My family and friends for listening to and laughing at all my stories all these years. But particularly my sister and father for passing on the funny bone and a love for writing to me. (Along with my sister's discarded baggy jeans and old stationery that made me look so cool at school.)

☆ The landlord who barged into my house and interrupted my phone interview for a very challenging job. If I had cleared the interview that day, I'd have

never found the time to write this book. (Now, can we not revise the rent this year?)
- ☆ The very loyal followers of my blogs and other public writings, who encouraged me to write a book. (I took your advice a bit too seriously there.)
- ☆ My sadistic school teacher of class five who made fun of the first poem I ever wrote and refused to include it in the school magazine. The poem talked about a bear that came to a town and went back. The end. In your face, Mrs…I am still scared to name her. I never stopped writing, and never will.

www.ingramcontent.com/pod-product-compliance
Lightning Source LLC
Chambersburg PA
CBHW030233170426

43201CB00006B/200